Writing about Music

An Introductory Guide

Richard J. Wingell
University of Southern California

PRENTICE HALL, Englewood Cliffs, New Jersey 07632

Library of Congress Cataloging-in-Publication Data

Wingell, Richard J.
    Writing about music : an introductory guide / Richard J. Wingell.
        p.   cm.
    Includes bibliographical references.
    ISBN 0-13-970856-1
    1. Music--Historiography--Handbooks, manuals, etc. 2. Musical
criticism--Authors'ip--Handbooks, manuals, etc. 3. Report writing-
-Handbooks, manuals, etc.   I. Title.
    ML3797.W54 1990
    780'.722--dc20
                                                        89-37939
                                                          CIP
                                                           MN

Editorial/production supervision and
  interior design: Carole Crouse
Cover design: Lorraine Mullaney
Manufacturing buyer: Raymond Keating/Michael Woerner

 © 1990 by Prentice-Hall, Inc.
A Division of Simon & Schuster
Englewood Cliffs, New Jersey 07632

Printed in the United States of America

10 9 8 7 6 5 4 3 2

ISBN 0-13-970856-1

PRENTICE-HALL INTERNATIONAL (UK) LIMITED, London
PRENTICE-HALL OF AUSTRALIA PTY. LIMITED, Sydney
PRENTICE-HALL CANADA INC., Toronto
PRENTICE-HALL HISPANOAMERICANA, S.A., Mexico
PRENTICE-HALL OF INDIA PRIVATE LIMITED, New Delhi
PRENTICE-HALL OF JAPAN, INC., Tokyo
SIMON & SCHUSTER ASIA PTE. LTD., Singapore
EDITORA PRENTICE-HALL DO BRASIL, LTDA., Rio de Janeiro

Contents

PART II   Writing a Research Paper on a Musical Topic

chapter 3

Getting Started: Research, 17

chapter 4

Writing a Research Paper, 30

chapter 5

Using a Word Processor to Produce a Paper, 43

chapter 6

Questions of Format, 48

PART III   Other Kinds of Writing about Music

chapter 7

The Seminar Presentation, 66

chapter 8

Program Notes, 72

chapter 9

Concert Reports, 79

chapter 10

Essay Examinations, 81

PART V   Conclusion

Conclusion, 125

appendix

Sample Paper, 127

Index, 143

Preface

This book is designed to serve as a guide to writing about music for undergraduate music majors. The idea for the book arose from the conviction that undergraduate music majors need such a guide for several reasons. Across the country, professors feel that today's undergraduate students cannot write convincing papers, not necessarily through any fault of their own, but because they have not been trained to write clear, coherent prose. Many students dread writing papers and put off writing assignments until the last possible second, when there is no time for anything but a slipshod job. Those professors who still assign term papers, convinced that writing research papers is an essential part of the experience of higher education, complain about reading stacks of dreary, illiterate papers. Some professors are so discouraged by the low level of student prose that they no longer even assign term papers, and they avoid essay questions in examinations, resorting instead to objective examinations made up entirely of short-answer questions. In some fields of study, it is possible to graduate, or even earn an advanced degree, without ever producing a substantial research paper.

At the present time, most college students have easy access to word-processing equipment. Some academics were convinced that the advent of the computer was a sign of the end of civilization as we know it; others assumed that in the new computer age student papers would be better edited and more of a pleasure to read. Both assumptions turned out to be wrong.

Some students use word-processing equipment to great advantage, while others do not understand how to use the powerful resources at their command and still hand in rough drafts, in sore need of editing, revision, and proofreading. Later in this book we will discuss the use of word-processing equipment in writing papers; many students apparently need some guidance about utilizing the amazing capabilities of word-processing equipment.

In general, then, according to most observers, the writing skills of college students are in a sorry state. The situation is even worse, many feel, in the field of music. As the educational system has become more specialized, musicians, like athletes, are identified and given professional training very early in their lives. While early training is an enormous advantage, the time devoted to the development of professional skills takes time away from the development of other kinds of academic skills. Many undergraduate music majors have never learned to write effective and convincing prose.

The problem is compounded further by the fact that it is inherently difficult to write about music. As we are well aware, music has an enormous power to move us, to delight us, to express deep feelings and longings. Like poetry, it can express subconscious or unconscious feelings much more effectively than prose can. It can be difficult, however, to describe what happens in the course of a musical work or to explain our responses to music in clear prose. Much of the writing we see about music avoids the challenge of speaking about musical events, preferring to discuss peripheral issues.

Thus, students of music, even those who have been blessed with solid training in writing, may have problems when faced with the task of writing about a musical topic. Others may need help with the basics of writing and a review of the appropriate language and format for college papers. This book attempts to provide practical assistance in both areas—writing effective prose and the special problems involved in writing about music. Obviously, a handbook of this size cannot hope to answer every possible question. The book will attempt to provide practical assistance in areas like writing about musical style, the research process, organizing a paper, general writing style, and common writing errors. The book will also direct the student to further resources.

OTHER RESOURCES AVAILABLE

This book is directed primarily to undergraduate music majors. There are several guides to musical research and writing at the graduate level, which discuss papers, theses, and dissertations. These guides may be helpful to undergraduate students as well, but many of the questions they discuss are not relevant to the undergraduate facing a term paper project. Among the resources at the graduate level are the following texts.

DUCKLES, VINCENT. *Music Reference and Research Materials: An Annotated Bibliography.* London: Free Press, 1964. Third edition, 1974.

HELM, EUGENE, and ALBERT T. LUPER. *Words and Music.* Hackensack, N.J.: J. Boonin, 1971. Revised edition, Totowa, N.J.: European-American Music, 1982.

IRVINE, DEMAR. *Writing about Music.* Seattle: University of Washington Press, 1956. Second edition, 1968.

WATANABE, RUTH T. *Introduction to Music Research.* Englewood Cliffs, N.J.: Prentice-Hall, 1967.

Watanabe's book and the Duckles bibliography, soon to appear in a fourth edition, are standard texts for graduate courses in research techniques. The books by Irvine and Helm and Luper are style guides that concentrate on the issues of style and format that arise in theses and dissertations.

There are also several standard guides to writing style. Although these works do not discuss the special problems involved in writing about music, they are helpful in matters of appropriate style and format for college papers. Among the best-known guides are the following texts.

The Chicago Manual of Style. Thirteenth edition. Chicago: Chicago University Press, 1982.

STRUNK, WILLIAM, and E. B. WHITE. *The Elements of Style.* New York: Macmillan, 1959. Second edition, 1972.

TROYKA, LYNN QUITMAN. *Simon & Schuster Handbook for Writers.* Third edition. Englewood Cliffs, N.J.: Prentice-Hall, 1990.

TURABIAN, KATE L. *A Manual for Writers of Term Papers, Theses, and Dissertations.* Chicago: University of Chicago Press, 1955. Third edition, 1967.

———. *Student's Guide for Writing College Papers.* Chicago: University of Chicago Press, 1963. Third edition, 1976.

Turabian's guides are standard reference works, recommended in many college and university courses. Although they do not deal with the special problems of writing about music, they are very helpful in other areas. The book by Strunk and White is an inexpensive paperback that discusses selected questions of writing style; it belongs in the personal library of anyone who cares about writing precise and careful English. The *Simon & Schuster Handbook* is a useful compendium of details of writing style. The *Chicago Manual* is a large, very detailed guide, a standard reference work for writers, editors, proofreaders, and publishers. It is the bible of the publishing world; the size of the book and the number of editions testify to its importance.

HOW TO USE THIS BOOK

This guide is not intended to be read cover to cover. It offers practical advice in several areas, including general writing problems as well as the special challenge of writing about music. Although it is aimed primarily at the undergraduate music major, nonmajors who are involved in music classes may find parts of it useful, and some graduate students may profit from a review of the process of writing a paper or the chapters on effective writing. Although some students may find some of the comments and suggestions surprisingly elementary, all the questions discussed, even the most basic ones, are included because they continue to cause problems for many students. Familiarize yourself with the book's organization, study the table of contents, and skim through the whole book so that you are aware of the areas that are covered. In the future, when you are involved in a writing project, you will be able to locate the material that may be of practical use to you.

The book is divided into four large sections. Part I (Chapters 1 and 2) discusses the issue of writing about music. Part II (Chapters 3–6) treats the research paper and discusses every stage of the process, from choosing a topic through outlining, writing the draft, editing and revising, and questions of format. Part III (Chapters 7–10) discusses other kinds of writing about music that you may be involved in—seminar presentations, program notes, concert reports, and essay examinations. Part IV (Chapters 11–14) treats writing in general—principles of style, effective writing, and common problems. The concluding section directs the reader to further readings and offers some last words of advice. In the Appendix is a sample paper. Skip around the book and use what you need. My hope is that all students will find helpful information somewhere in this book. If not, it should direct them to other resources where they can find the help they seek.

SOME BASIC IDEAS ABOUT WRITING

Because of my experience reading hundreds of student papers and my own experience with various kinds of writing, including articles for scholarly journals, textbooks, program notes, and some attempts at writing fiction, I have become convinced of some basic truths about writing.

1. *Effective writing is a learned skill, not an inborn talent.* It is frustrating to hear a student say, "I've always been a poor speller," with a shrug, as if an inability to spell were a charming imperfection, over which the student has no control. Writing precise and correct prose is hard work, but there is no particular mystery about it. Anyone can learn to write clear and forceful prose.

2. The second principle follows from the first. *Anyone can improve his or her writing skills.* One does not need special courses, tutors, or technical training to hone one's writing skills. Even leading scholars and important writers sometimes produce prose that is less than perfect; much of the material we read each day could be improved by further revising and editing. Good writers work harder than you might imagine to make the

words say exactly what they want to say, and they constantly work to improve their writing style.

3. *The first and most important step toward improving your writing is to develop the attitude that your writing matters and that it deserves care, effort, and precision.* I find it shocking that some students have no qualms about handing in shoddy papers filled with typographical errors and grammatical blunders that would shame a sixth-grader. Often it is obvious that these papers were typed in a rush the night before the deadline, often by friends with no musical background, who had no idea of what they were typing. One wonders what these students' recitals would be like if they were as unprofessional about their performances as they are about their papers. The performers would arrive a half-hour late, or perhaps on the wrong evening altogether, wearing their most casual clothes, yawning, scratching, and fumbling around for music stands and their parts. Music majors find that picture ludicrous—of course they know how to dress and behave when presenting a public performance. They follow accepted recital customs, whether they believe in them or not, because they know that they must if they expect to establish their professional competence. They should take the same attitude toward their papers. English spelling may be difficult and illogical, and some of the rules about acceptable format may seem silly, but spelling does count in life, and there is a correct way to present a paper, just as there is acceptable recital deportment. If you want to be taken seriously as a student, you must learn how to write an acceptable paper.

4. *There are different types of writing, each with its own standards and rules.* What might be perfectly appropriate in poetry or fiction, or in a letter to a friend, may not be suitable in a research paper. Research papers are regarded as "technical writing," as opposed to journalism, poetry, or fiction. The standards of technical writing are clear, consistent, universally accepted, and easy enough to learn.

5. *One can improve one's writing in several ways.* First, *read*. Read all sorts of writing—fiction, essays, history, biography. Turn off the television and read for pleasure when you have a spare moment. Read critically, with an eye to appreciating good style. Second, *write*. The only way to learn how to write is to write and rewrite—first write a draft, then revise, edit, cut, polish, get critical opinions from reliable critics, and continue rewriting. There are no shortcuts to producing a first-quality paper, any more than there are shortcuts to a good performance. If you start writing your paper the night before it is due, you can rest assured that it will not be a first-class paper. If, on the other hand, you allow time for the difficult work of editing, rewriting, tightening, polishing, and proofreading, then your paper is much more likely to be an accomplishment of which you can be proud, something that does justice to the time you put into the research, and something that establishes your competence and professionalism.

CONCLUSION

This book is intended to serve as a practical introductory guide. It does not pretend to present the last word on all issues involved in writing about music. Rather, it is intended to be helpful in a few important areas, especially to the student facing the task of writing a paper on a musical topic. If the book helps a handful of students to produce papers that are stronger, clearer, and more convincing, it will have justified its existence. If it means that a professor somewhere will read a stack of papers in which a larger proportion are a pleasure to read, and fewer are illiterate, then the book will have succeeded in its purpose

Finally, I should thank some people who, wittingly or unwittingly, supplied ideas and material for this book. First, I am indebted to Norwell F. Therien, Jr., Senior Humanities Editor of Prentice-Hall, who first conceived the idea for this book and worked closely with every phase of this project. Next, I thank my colleagues in Music History at the University of Southern California, who over the years have shared with me examples of poor writing produced by their classes. Finally, I must thank the hundreds of students whose papers I have read and who have contributed to this book, directly or indirectly. I also thank the writers whose prose I have paraphrased in the examples of poor writing. I have not quoted these examples verbatim or identified the authors. The authors whose work I admire and offer as examples of fine writing are named and credited in the text.

Richard J. Wingell

chapter 1

Writing about Music

WHY WE WRITE ABOUT MUSIC

Throughout the history of music, there have always been those who resist the idea of discussing music or writing about it. These people feel that music speaks for itself and that it is impossible to describe musical events in words. Even in the nineteenth century, with all its artistic manifestos, arguments about the directions music should take, and endless discussions of music's capacity to depict stories or philosophical ideas, there were still those who insisted that music should speak for itself and that writing about it was foolish. In our own day, many composers resist the attempts of commentators to explain their music, preferring to let the music speak for them. Aside from having to produce a paper to satisfy the requirements of a class, why would someone go to the effort of writing about this complex and difficult art? Why do some professors feel it is important to assign writing projects on musical topics? What purpose is served by crafting clear prose about music?

Sometimes the purpose of writing about music is clear and straightforward. When one writes program notes, for example, the goal is to help the audience understand the music better and thus increase their enjoyment of the concert. Sometimes one writes about music in order to establish one's credentials as a knowledgeable musician. It seems obvious that a performer who can speak intelligently of the historical background and style of a piece of music is a more competent musician than a performer who may be able to play the notes, but who cannot say anything intelligent about the music beyond "I like it," "I don't like it," or "It's hard to play." Further, one might write about a piece of music in order to demonstrate one's analytic understanding of how the work is put together, what gives it coherence, logic, and syntax. Professors often assign writing projects to see if the student can apply the ideas discussed in class to other musical works, a more thoughtful and demanding task than simply absorbing and repeating in an examination what the professor has said. Papers are exercises in what psychologists call second-order learning—that is, the ability to apply new information and skills. Finally, one might write about music in order to convey the results of one's historical or biographical research on a musical topic. Musicological research is concerned with other areas besides analysis; it also includes studies in biography, cultural background, connections with the other arts, performance practice issues, and other topics that affect the course of music history.

THE SPECIAL CHALLENGES OF WRITING ABOUT MUSIC

The Preface alluded to the special difficulties of writing convincingly about music. Music is a nonverbal art; it often seems to speak directly to feelings deep within us that are difficult to put into words. For that reason, music has always been a crucial part of religious rituals, patriotic ceremonies, and solemn occasions, civic or private. Even when music accompanies a text, as in art song or opera, we find it difficult to express exactly what the music "says" beyond what the text says, or what the music adds to the words. Often we feel that a musical setting captures the feeling of a text with remarkable exactness, that it is exactly "right" for that text, but it is difficult to explain that conviction in prose. The very nature of music resists attempts to verbalize about it. On the other hand, when we finally arrive at a clear vision of a work, or when we have strong ideas about a work's uniqueness or historical importance, we want to communicate those ideas and opinions. Words are the only means we have to communicate what we want to say about music.

Besides the inherent difficulty of writing about music, there are extrinsic factors that make it more difficult. There are many performers who seem to approach all music simply as a challenge to their technique, as if the only important music consisted of solos for their particular instrument. Their attitude seems to be, "Spare me the lectures—give me the score and I'll take it home and learn it." It is astonishing that so many fine players, professionals of great skill and sensitivity, not only know so little about the music they play, but also seem to have little interest in changing that situation. Perhaps they learned that attitude from their teachers; unfortunately, some continue to teach technique alone, without analytic or stylistic understanding.

Outside the world of musicians, society's attitudes toward music affect us. Society treats music as comforting background, an atmosphere one creates for oneself, a sort of sonic wallpaper. In this view, no one has any right to question anyone else's musical taste; like religion or politics, musical taste is regarded as a personal matter and a dangerous area to discuss. Many people cannot imagine that there is a level of discussion possible beyond rudimentary approval or disapproval. In this atmosphere, it is difficult to argue logically and convincingly about issues of musical style and quality.

INAPPROPRIATE WAYS TO WRITE ABOUT MUSIC

Because it is difficult to write about music, some writers fill their pages with irrelevant discussions, resorting to diversionary tactics in order to avoid the challenge of actually discussing the music. We have all read examples of such approaches to writing about music; some of us may even have been responsible for producing prose of this sort. I mention these approaches not to ridicule them but to be clear about tendencies that we want to eliminate from our own writing. Please note that the words I cite as examples of bad writing are not direct quotations but paraphrases of prose I have read.

Sometimes, especially in program notes and record liner notes, one finds overly precious descriptions of musical events, sentences like the following.

> The violas insist on interrupting with their own little theme, but the woodwinds are not impressed, and continue chattering among themselves. Finally, the brasses put a stop to the argument by drowning out everyone else and restoring order.

That sort of nonsense need not detain us for long; it says nothing about the music and, instead, adopts a precious tone, personalizes the instruments, and becomes childish rather than informative.

I recently read a description of a slow introduction to the first movement of a classical symphony that went something like this:

> The introduction is nonthematic, but provides a delightful *aperitif* to the movement proper.

The writer gives us this fanciful comparison because he cannot think of anything worthwhile to say about the music.

Sometimes, sentimental or overly picturesque descriptions take the place of serious discussion. Returning themes "dispel the gloom and chaos of the preceding section," or "The light of hope dawns anew as we approach the triumphant final cadence." Themes "babble," "chatter," "argue," "soar," or "shout." This picturesque rhetoric provides little of substance to the reader who wants to understand the music.

Another tendency is to treat all music as programmatic, regardless of the style in question or the composer's intent. It is perfectly all right to let one's imagination wander and conjure up colorful pictures or scenes as one listens to music, even absolute or abstract music. It would be interesting if we could see what passes through the minds of concert audiences during a performance. Reporting on one's fantasies, however, hardly fulfills the writer's responsibility to discuss musical style in a serious paper. One student, in a paper analyzing a concerto grosso, included the information that Baroque music always conjured up images of royal processions in her mind. That bit of shared information is not relevant to the discussion.

There is a nineteenth-century description of the opening of Brahms's First Symphony that goes on at some length about "the cosmic questions posed by the philosophic C." The opening of that symphony is certainly one of the most dramatic opening gestures in the symphonic literature, but "cosmic questions"? What makes that opening effective is the relentless pounding of the pedal C while the orchestra moves away from its initial unison C by chromatic steps in contrary motion. That last sentence may not be the most elegant description of Brahms's opening, but at least it tells the reader something about what happens in the music.

Related to the programmatic tendency is the approach that tries to explain all music through events in the composer's life. Beethoven's deafness, for example, occupies altogether too much space in discussions of his later music; it is easier to write about his affliction than to discuss the puzzling style of his late works. There is a published discussion of Mozart's Piano Concerto in B-flat, K. 595, that relates this last concerto to Mozart's supposed feelings as he neared the end of his short life. The writer describes the serene slow movement as "suffused with the soft glow of evening," or words to that effect, and hears resignation and a longing for death in every note. The connection with Mozart's feelings in his last days is hard to justify, since many of his earlier slow movements are equally serene. Besides, Mozart hardly seems the sort of person who would approach his untimely death with an "evening glow" of resignation. Nineteenth-century writers loved to treat Mozart as a tragic Romantic hero. The emphasis on the tragic side of his life tells us little about Mozart's real genius or about his music. Sometimes details of a composer's life, such as an important friendship or a new position, can shed helpful light on his musical style. One must always bear in mind, however, that unhappy composers can write happy music and that composers whose lives are dull can write turbulent, passionate music. Examples come to mind readily. Bartók's *Concerto for Orchestra* hardly sounds like the work of a composer who was dying of leukemia in an American hospital, impoverished, exiled from war-torn Europe, depressed, and discouraged. Richard Strauss in his private life was, we are told, a henpecked, middle-class German, but his tone poems embody all the sweep, grandeur, and ardent heroism of late Romanticism.

These approaches to writing about music are obviously inadequate; there are other inappropriate approaches that deserve mention before we go on to what writing about music *should* do.

Some students think they have said all there is to say about a piece of music when they have reported the musical events in the order in which they occur. You surely have read prose of this sort.

The first sixteen measures of the development section are based on the first theme, and gradually reduce the musical idea to the opening flourish, which then moves through several keys. The next thirty-two measures continue the modulatory process, after which a dominant pedal prepares for the recapitulation.

While this "one-thing-after-another" approach appears to be neutral, objective, and scientific, it is not real analysis, as we shall see later. Unless the music happens to be organized as a series of unrelated events, as in some twentieth-century styles, compiling a list of events avoids taking a position on what is important in the music, what unifies the work and gives it coherence, and what makes it different from other works in the same genre. The listing of musical events is certainly a vast improvement over gushing prose about babbling brooks, chattering woodwinds, the imagined feelings of the composer at the time, or the dreams of the listener's imagination. It is only a beginning, however, and does not adequately discuss the music.

Another common error is anachronistic analysis—using the analytic tools and categories appropriate to one style of music or to one era to describe music of a different era, or forcing music through the wrong stylistic mold. The concepts of structure and key areas that work for analyzing Haydn symphonies will not be of much use in analyzing the Machaut Mass or aleatoric music by John Cage. Students often try to analyze early music by using the standard-practice analytic terms and categories that they have recently learned. When grappling with music that does not have antecedent and consequent phrases, clear key areas, and familiar classical forms, they sometimes try to force the music to fit the wrong style. The next chapter, on stylistic analysis, will discuss this issue in more detail.

For now, we can summarize the point of this section in one sentence: Writing about music should focus on the music. Silly, fanciful, and overly imaginative descriptions of music are beside the point, as are descriptions that base everything on details, real or imagined, of the composer's life. All these approaches sidestep the real task, which is to write about what happens in the music. In your own writing about music, the most important goal is to avoid these traps and to face squarely the challenge of writing as thoughtfully and as clearly as you can about the music.

The first step toward writing about a musical work is understanding that work in its own terms and seeing where the individual work fits within its genre and style. In other words, the first step is careful analysis, the topic of the next chapter.

chapter 2

Stylistic Analysis

Before one can write clearly about a musical work, one must first understand that work—how it is organized, what gives it unity and coherence, and which elements are critical in creating that particular musical statement. One reaches that understanding through the process called analysis. Not everyone defines analysis in the same way; historians generally take a developmental view of analysis, viewing the individual work against the background of evolving historical styles. A good explanation of stylistic analysis is *Guidelines for Style Analysis* by Jan La Rue (New York: W. W. Norton & Co., 1970).

It is important to realize that analysis is not an exact science, with quantifiable issues and definite answers. In this century, several new approaches to musical analysis have emerged, such as the systems of Heinrich Schenker, Paul Hindemith, and Allen Forte, each with its own contribution to the understanding of past and present music. Many of the new methods of analysis emphasize the structure of a work or its materials and methods rather than its style. These systems can offer valuable insights into music of any period. The final test of any analysis, whatever its methodology or goals, is listening to the music. Music, after all, consists of sounds, not marks on a page. Any valid analysis should therefore make sense and increase our understanding of the work as we listen to it.

DEFINITION

In theory courses, the term *analysis* usually refers either to harmonic and structural analysis of pieces from the so-called standard-practice period, from 1750 to 1900, or to new systems of analysis developed in the twentieth century. Music historians generally use the term to mean stylistic analysis, and they study musical works in terms of changing historical styles. All composers work within a stylistic context; they either accept the conventions of the style of their time or work against those conventions, creating new musical styles. Therefore, meaningful analysis ought to be based on a clear understanding of the stylistic developments that formed the context in which a particular work appeared. We cannot appreciate the unique aspects of a particular work until we understand the principles that guide the music of the period. Therefore, musicology often concentrates its effort on defining clearly the principles of a particular style.

No matter how one defines analysis, it certainly involves more than mere description, chord counting, or a listing of events. An approach based on "first this happens, then this happens, then something else happens" is not true analysis, unless the work happens to be organized, as in some twentieth-century styles, as a series of juxtaposed but otherwise unrelated events. Analysis implies insight into how the music is conceived and organized. To reach that insight, one may have to start with list-making activities, such as identifying repetitions of thematic material, sorting out key areas, marking cadences and their relative finality, or identifying and listing the various sections of the work. These activities, however, are only the preliminaries to analysis; after events are identified and sorted out, the real work of analysis begins. One must decide which events are significant and how the work relates to a more general historical style. Then one can decide which elements of the work are standard practice for the time and which are innovative. In other words, analysis is not a totally objective activity; it involves a creative mind and artistic judgment, as well as the ability to create an analytic hypothesis and the appropriate means to test that hypothesis.

In a similar vein, analysis of a musical work is different from understanding the compositional process involved. To understand a Renaissance Mass, for example, it is important to know whether the work is based on a *cantus firmus*, to identify the *cantus firmus*, and to study the ways in which the composer has used the preexisting melody in the various movements of the Mass, including devices such as augmentation, diminution, and retrograde. But that understanding is only the first step and does not fully describe the musical style. Using the same compositional process, composers like Dufay, Ockeghem, and Josquin produced *cantus firmus* Masses that are stylistically quite distinct, since the three composers treated elements like rhythm, texture, phrase length, imitation, and vertical effects in different ways. All three worked within the well-defined style of Renaissance sacred choral music, but a trained ear can recognize the stylistic differences in the works of these composers.

Similarly, the laborious task of locating all the permutations of the row in a twelve-tone work is different from stylistic analysis. Schoenberg's twelve-tone works are stylistically quite distinct from those of Berg, Webern, or Boulez. The issue of compositional process may sometimes be irrelevant to the question of style, since the structure and coherence of a work often result from entirely different considerations. Many of Schoenberg's twelve-tone works, for example, are organized in recognizable versions of classical structures, like sonata-allegro or rondo; the seams between sections are often articulated through familiar classical means, such as melodic and rhythmic cadence, change of texture, or change of instrumentation, which have nothing to do with row permutations. Knowledge of the compositional process can certainly shed light on the organization of a work. In the two styles just described, the compositional process may provide the work's unity and coherence, since the common material is the basis of the extended work. Still, the task of analysis involves more than awareness of compositional process.

Analysis, then, is something other than harmonic and structural analysis of works from the standard-practice period, making lists, or understanding the compositional process. Most historians would define analysis as *insight into how a work is organized, what gives it logic and coherence, and how it relates to the important stylistic developments of its time.*

QUESTIONS TO CONSIDER

To begin the process of musical analysis, one should consider several basic questions. Is this particular work organized as a coherent unit? If so, what is the basis of its coherence? What makes this work a unified whole? Is it based on one of the traditional structural patterns, like sonata-allegro, minuet and trio, or theme and variations, or does it have some other form? We can assume that musical works are based on some principle of organization; unless we sense some logic and coherence in a work, no matter how unusual the principle of organization, we tend to dismiss it as random and unmusical. *Identifying the musical means by which the composer has built in unity and coherence is the most important step in analysis.*

A basic question in stylistic analysis is how a particular work relates to the stylistic developments of its time. Is it a venture into completely new territory, or does it build on established styles? Is it a further refinement of a style in which the composer has worked previously, or is he experimenting with new stylistic ideas? In what way has he worked out his own version of an established style? Further, is there evidence that the composer was influenced by another composer? Claims of another composer's influence are difficult to support; similarity of style is not enough in itself to justify such a claim, since there are several other possible explanations for such similarity. The line of influence may run in the opposite direction, or both may have been influenced by a third composer or by a pervasive style of that period. Influence is hard to prove from the music alone unless we have the composer's own words or some other historical evidence that establishes a connection. Within these limits, however, the question of influence and the other general questions listed earlier are ways to approach the crucial issue of where a work fits in the overall history of a style.

A third approach to beginning an analysis project is to relate a particular work to the surrounding culture and contemporary developments in the other arts. At some points in history, the connections between music and the other arts are particularly obvious. French art songs of the early twentieth century, for example, cannot be understood without reference to the symbolist movement in literature, which produced the evocative texts that influenced the composers' musical choices and led them to create a new musical style. Likewise, the songs of Schoenberg and Berg cannot be understood without some understanding of the expressionist movement in German art and literature. In fact, we often use terms borrowed from the world of the visual arts, like impressionism and expressionism, to describe musical styles, and we cannot discuss expressionism in music without first understanding what the term means in its original context. Programmatic music clearly cannot be analyzed without some reference to the story or picture that the music is trying to depict.

The question of cultural context is much broader than those musical styles that are obviously influenced by the visual or literary arts. The physical setting in which music was performed, the audience for whom it was intended, the context in which music was performed, and the way a particular society viewed the role of composer or performer all affect questions of stylistic development. Understanding a musical work may involve research into these sociological questions. We need to be aware of concert life in earlier ages, the performing forces composers had at their disposal, and the context in which music was performed. In order to understand the cantatas of Bach, for example, we should first understand that they were designed to be performed as part of the Sunday services of a particular church, in an era whose sense of piety was warm and personal. The better we understand the original purpose of a musical work, the audience for whom it was intended, and the circumstances of its first performance, the better prepared we are to make sense of the music.

THE INTENT OF THE COMPOSER

Another fundamental question to raise in the early stages of an analysis project is the composer's intent. Composers write their music for many different reasons, and understanding their motivation may very well be the key to understanding the music they produce.

Sometimes a composer writes music for a particular occasion, and that special purpose affects the style of the music he writes. A famous example is the motet *Nuper rosarum flores* by Guillaume Dufay, one of the masterpieces of the early Renaissance. The piece is remarkably complex and utilizes two isorhythmic tenors, following a compositional process borrowed from the French Ars Nova. One can, of course, analyze the motet by working from the score alone, but it makes more sense to see the work in its historical context. The motet was commissioned for the dedication in 1436 of the new cathedral in Florence, the famous "Duomo." This ceremony was an important occasion in Renaissance Italy; the Pope traveled to the city of the Medicis for the ceremony, and it was an honor to be asked to write music for this historic occasion. Recent scholarship has established that the double-tenor structure of Dufay's piece was intended to celebrate the architectural boldness of the large unsupported dome designed by Brunelleschi. The two tenors are arranged in a mathematical proportion that mirrors the proportions of the dome. In other words, the circumstances explain the structure of the music, and it would be a mistake to deal with this piece as if it were a typical motet.

Composers have often written music for a particular performer, and that circumstance should help us understand those works. Compositional choices may be based on the talents of the performers for whom the works are intended, and the question of instrumental idiom may be the most important question to raise in the analytical process.

Sometimes the composer's main purpose is to experiment with new materials or structures. Much of the music composed since 1945 should be approached with a clear awareness of the composer's purpose. George Crumb, for example, has discussed his desire to combine ideas borrowed from Oriental music, ritual, astronomy, and drama in his music. Works of this period, in which the composer often creates a new style or structure for a single work, must be analyzed in terms of what he intended to accomplish. If a composer has organized a particular work around mathematical structures, has ordered all the elements serially, or has integrated musical ideas from other cultures into Western structures, we cannot analyze or appreciate the work except in those terms.

Sometimes, on the other hand, a composer may be refining an established style, and the key to analyzing his work is to view it against the background of that established style. That is the case with much of the music from the standard-practice period. When we approach a Mozart symphony, we know how to proceed because we have some understanding of the principles of classical structure. When a composer moves from one style to another, as Stravinsky did in his later years, we obviously have to be aware of that change and must not try to analyze his serial works in the same way as his neoclassical works.

Finally, if a composer has written a programmatic work, we must judge the music in those terms, and we cannot adequately appreciate the music without some understanding of the program. The same holds true for text setting in song and opera; the complex relationship between text and music is one of the major questions to consider in the process of analysis.

In short, we should judge musical works against the background of what the composer was trying to do. To ignore available information about the composer's intent is to deprive ourselves of useful information about the directions the analysis should take. Sometimes we are already armed with an understanding of the composer's intent, as in the case of Mozart or Beethoven. In other cases, we may have to begin our analysis by study of the background and historical context of the composer so that we can approach his music as he approached it and avoid using inappropriate criteria in our study of the work.

It is difficult to generalize about the process of analysis, because one approaches different styles of music in different ways. Rather than extending this general discussion of analytical principles, we should now look at some specific works and discuss approaches that would be fruitful in understanding these particular works.

EXAMPLES OF ANALYTICAL APPROACHES

The basic point of stylistic analysis is that no single analytic system works equally well for all music; one must analyze a work against the background of its particular style. Therefore, we will now look briefly at some specific works and discuss ways to approach the task of analyzing them. These works are readily available in standard anthologies of music and certainly can be found in any music library. It would be helpful to have the scores at hand as you read this section, so that you can follow the discussion and decide for yourself which approaches seem most fruitful.

Gesualdo: *Moro, lasso*

This famous madrigal is an example of Gesualdo's idiosyncratic style. As you first glance at the score, several aspects of the musical style strike you immediately. The first is the strange chromaticism in the setting of certain phrases—"Moro, lasso," "ahi, che m'ancide," "O dolorosa sorte," and "ahi, mi da morte." We know that the sixteenth-century Italian madrigal in its later stages was concerned with musical rhetoric—that is, finding striking musical ways to depict the individual words of the text. Clearly, one fruitful way to approach this piece is from the point of view of text setting, starting with the words of the Italian poem and considering each example of word painting. The words "Moro, lasso," for example, are set to a chromatically descending phrase in the low range, suitable for the words "I die, I languish." These chordal chromatic sections alternate with polyphonic phrases in diatonic style, which depict the more hopeful lines like "e chi me può dar vita" ("she who could give me life").

You might also focus on the details of the chromatic passages—for example, the composer's tendency to combine chromatic descent with what we would call root movement by thirds. The chromatic passages might also be discussed in terms of the modal theory of the time. You might also focus on the question of overall structure. Note that alternation of two different styles and repetition of contrasting passages create the large structure; you might argue the question of unity and coherence versus the contrasting momentary effects. However you proceed, the question of text setting and "madrigalisms" would be an important one.

J. S. Bach: Cantata No. 80, *Ein' feste Burg ist unser Gott,* Opening Chorus

The most important principle of organization in this chorus, as is usually the case in the choruses of Bach's chorale cantatas, is the relationship between the traditional chorale melody and the complex counterpoint that Bach builds from it. Analysis must begin with the chorale tune with which Bach began; it is found in the soprano line of the final number of the cantata. The key to the structure of the first chorus is that Bach uses the chorale tune in two different ways. First, the choral parts constitute a *chorale motet;* that is, Bach uses each phrase of the chorale tune as a subject for imitative entries in all the voices. This is an old technique, one we associate with the motets of Josquin. The melody is not quoted literally but given new rhythmic shape and amplified by added notes, just as Renaissance composers altered chant melodies when they used them as imitative subjects in their motets. At the end of each imitative section, the orchestra presents the same phrase of the chorale in literal form, in long notes—what is called *cantus firmus* style. In addition, these literal quotations of the chorale phrases in long notes are set canonically between the top and bottom instruments of the orchestra, at a distance of one measure. Once one understands the two ways of quoting the phrases of the chorale, one understands the whole chorus, since Bach continues this process throughout the chorus. Read through the chorus and see if you can follow the progress of the chorale motet; the orchestra's quotations of the chorale phrases in *cantus firmus* style clearly mark the end of each imitative section. The structure of the chorus duplicates the A A B structure of the chorale. Other questions one might consider are the relationship of this huge first chorus to the overall structure of the cantata and the other movements, or the question of different editions—compare the *Bach-Gesell-schaft* edition of this chorus to the version in the *Neue Bach-Ausgabe*. One might also contrast this chorus with an opening chorus organized differently, like the first chorus of Cantata No. 4, *Christ lag in Todesbanden*.

Mozart: Piano Concerto in C Minor, K. 491, First Movement

In this work, the student is on the familiar ground of standard-practice analysis. Here one works with familiar elements like key areas, thematic repetition, the development process, and classical structures. What this particular movement illustrates is the variety possible within standard classical forms. Structural analysis shows that this movement does not follow the double-exposition version of sonata-allegro structure that some textbooks describe as typical of the first movement of a classical concerto. Many commentators view this movement as an example of *ritornello* form rather than a sonata-allegro structure. Look through the whole movement. Does the solo piano ever play the first theme? Do the key areas work out as you would expect in a classical sonata-allegro movement in the minor mode? Structure seems to be the logical focus for an analysis of this movement; other interesting areas for investigation are the questions of instrumental idiom and orchestration. Some commentators view this particular concerto as an example of Mozart's darker, Beethovenian side, in contrast to the sunnier, gentler spirit of some of his other piano concertos. A comparative analysis, contrasting this concerto with another one, perhaps the Concerto in A Major, K. 488, would be an interesting project.

Verdi: *Otello*, Act 1, Scene 3

The love duet between Otello and Desdemona at the end of Act 1 of Verdi's *Otello* is both stunning music and effective theater. The opera opens with Otello's triumphant return from a victory over the Turks; a celebration follows, during which Iago sets the plot in motion by getting Cassio drunk and involved in a fight so that Otello will punish him with imprisonment. Then everyone else leaves the stage, and Desdemona welcomes home her triumphant lover. The extended love scene that closes the act is one of the high points of the opera and could be studied from several points of view. The musical style is richer and more complex than the style we associate with Verdi's earlier operas. We are immediately struck by the delicately beautiful orchestration, which is filled with unusual effects. The harmonic idiom, marked by frequent modulations and enharmonic shifts, is also striking. Although some commentators see the structure of a traditional *scena* in this duet, the music seems more continuous and flowing than in his earlier works. The climax of the scene is the "un bacio" motive, which will return at the tragic close of the opera.

Besides discussion of these musical details, there are other approaches you might consider. Some writers see a shift in style between Verdi's late works, *Otello* and *Falstaff*, and his earlier works. A comparative analysis might try to identify common stylistic traits in these two works and contrast them with an earlier work. Another fascinating issue is the way the characters change and the story's emphasis shifts because of the changes Boito made in the process of adapting Shakespeare's play as a libretto. Although this last question may seem more literary than musical, it does involve musical analysis, since an opera has its own formal shape and structural laws. When Boito and Verdi adapted the play, which has its own structure and flow, into another medium, change was inevitable. You might also compare this adaptation with Verdi's other adaptations of Shakespeare's plays—*Macbeth* and *Falstaff*.

Liszt: *Faust Symphony*, First Movement

The *Faust Symphony* of Liszt is a masterpiece of Romantic program music and a fascinating work to analyze. The three movements represent the three main characters of the Faust legend—Faust, Gretchen, and Mephistopheles. Added to the final movement is an apotheosis, during which a male chorus and a soloist sing the last few lines of Goethe's *Faust*.

One important element in this work is the technique of thematic transformation. All the themes of the long first movement are derived from a few germs, or motives; as these germs are given different musical shape, they turn into themes, or leitmotifs, that represent the different sides of the hero—mystery, heroism, ardent love, and so on. One fruitful approach would be to focus on the germ motives and their different thematic versions. Another interesting study would be to compare the first and third movements, since most of the themes representing Mephistopheles are parodies of the Faust themes; in other words, the germ ideas that are manipulated and transformed in the first movement are further transformed in the final movement to depict completely different ideas. Another analysis might focus on the question of structure. This movement is very long and it sometimes rambles; the question of underlying structure in a Romantic movement of this size is an interesting one. Other important elements for analysis include harmonic language and orchestration.

Stravinsky: *The Rite of Spring*, Opening Sections

Although *The Rite of Spring* is a classic work of the early twentieth century, it calls for analytical methods that are somewhat different from those appropriate for music of the eighteenth and nineteenth centuries. In this landmark work, according to some commentators, Stravinsky re-arranged the elements of music and their relative importance in order to create a style appropriate to the story and the ballet. Rhythm is all-important, melody less so; the few tunes in this section, borrowed from Russian folk music, are fragmentary, narrow-range motives that repeat obsessively. *Ostinato* techniques and increasing thickness of texture take the place of traditional development. Instruments are used in new ways; the whole orchestra is sometimes used as a large percussion section. Form is articulated through rhythm and orchestration as much as through melodic material or harmonic cadences. Analysis of this work must begin by understanding the succession of musical events rather than by looking for traditional forms. The historical importance of this work comes from the fact that, while its purpose is a nineteenth-century one—it is, after all, program music designed to accompany a ballet—its musical means are in some ways new.

You might focus an analytic study of this work on the new elements or on the traditional aspects of the work. It would also be fruitful to compare it to its predecessors, *The Firebird* and *Petrushka*, in order to isolate the new elements in this work. In any case, *The Rite of Spring* is certainly a work that demands to be studied on its own terms.

Finally, note that these brief comments do not pretend to be models of analysis or exhaustive lists of ways to approach these works. Perhaps Schenker reductive analysis or set theory might turn out to be the most illuminating approach. My remarks are intended only as preliminary indications of directions you might take in analyzing these works. Each work must be studied in ways that illuminate its particular organization. In one sense, stylistic analysis is a circular process. Its goal is the understanding of a musical style, but one cannot begin the analysis until one has enough awareness of the style to be able to choose appropriate methods of analysis. An analysis that asks the wrong questions or searches for stylistic characteristics that are not there will never produce insight into the organization and coherence of that work. At the start of an analytic project, one may need to put aside the specific work for a while and first develop an awareness of the stylistic context from which it came.

Not every research paper for a class in music needs to be analytical in design and purpose, but sooner or later one must write about musical analysis. The most critical skill for effective writing about music, on any level, is the ability to analyze a musical work. No matter how skillful and forceful one's writing may be, one will not be able to write effectively about music without a well-developed ability to understand an individual musical work on its own terms and in the context of the stylistic developments of its time.

chapter 3

Getting Started: Research

This chapter will discuss the first phase of the process of producing a paper on a musical topic—the research phase. Naturally, the process will vary greatly, depending on the topic; not everything we discuss will be relevant to every project. In this chapter we will discuss basic resources, places to start, rather than the resources for highly specialized research. For specialized research, consult the texts designed for graduate researchers listed in the Preface, especially the Watanabe book and the Duckles bibliography. Here we are more concerned with the *process* of research and, especially, how to get started on an undergraduate research project.

CHOOSING A TOPIC

In many undergraduate classes, choosing a topic may not be an issue for the student; often the professor assigns a single topic for the whole class. When you do have to choose a topic, the following considerations may be helpful.

When the project is first discussed, you need to have a clear idea of the kind of paper the professor has in mind. Either the handout explaining the assignment or the discussion in class should make the professor's expectations clear, so that you do not waste time designing projects that will not be acceptable. The time to ask questions about acceptable topics is when the assignment is first discussed. Sometimes students do not listen closely to the explanation of the assignment, assuming that they need not worry about their papers until much later in the semester. A week before the paper is due, these students suddenly appear, seeking approval for unsuitable topics, and then have to scramble to put together something appropriate.

Once you understand what sort of topic is expected, you need to choose a general research area and then narrow that area down to a specific topic. One way to select a topic is to think first in terms of genre and then specific repertoire. If the class covers baroque music, for example, you might first decide whether you want to work with instrumental or vocal music. If you choose the vocal area, you can then select from the various genres—for example, opera, cantata, sacred concerto, or oratorio. If you decide on opera, then you must choose from the various styles—Florentine, Venetian, Neapolitan, French, German, and English. Then choose a specific time period, composer, and work. Another way to select a topic is to start with a particular time period or geographical area and find a suitable topic related to that time and place. There are many ways to choose a topic; the important thing is to begin making that decision early in the semester, long before the project is due.

At this point, students usually need to do some preliminary browsing in the music library to see what scores and recordings are available and what the secondary literature has to say. By "secondary literature" we mean reference books, histories, biographies, articles, or anything published by later commentators, as opposed to "primary" sources—the manuscripts, early prints, and similar materials from the period you are studying. There is little point in choosing an attractive topic if there are no scores available and nothing has been written about the topic in the secondary sources. If it becomes clear that investigating a topic would involve sending for microfilms of unpublished materials from a European library or spending three months in a European archive, you might want to choose another topic.

Once you have decided on a topic, clear your idea with the professor before going much further with your research. Do not waste valuable time working on a topic that is not acceptable or one that the professor knows will not be suitable for an undergraduate project.

When you are trying to move from a general area to a more specific topic, it is easy to identify the significant composers in that style. Your music history textbook can give you some help; later in this chapter we will discuss other general resources that are helpful in these early stages. The main thing in choosing a topic is to select something specific enough to be realistic as a topic for a paper, without getting so specific that you have problems with availability of materials, or moving into levels of research for which you are not qualified. "The Symphonies of Haydn," for example, is too broad a topic for a term paper. In a fifteen-page paper, you might be able to list all the symphonies and write a sentence or two about each, but the result would be a general summary, another version of the brief discussions already available in the secondary literature. On the other hand, you are not expected at this stage to solve highly technical research problems, like determining whether an obscure work is actually the work of Haydn; that is the sort of research problem better left to experienced scholars. There are several possibilities in between these two extremes. You might choose to compare an early symphony with a later one, determining through comparative analysis how Haydn's style changed over the course of his career. You might focus on a few first movements, comparing different versions of the sonata-allegro process. You might concentrate on the question of structure in a few slow movements. There are hundreds of fine topics within the general area of Haydn symphonies; it takes some thought and some preliminary work with the scores and the secondary sources to find a topic that will work for you. Since you will spend considerable time working on whatever topic you choose, be sure that you have a topic you like, a topic you are qualified to deal with, and a plan that you can carry through to a successful conclusion.

Kinds of Topics

Most research papers fall into a few standard types; as you think about possible topics, it may be helpful to think in terms of these standard types.

One common type of topic focuses on analysis of a single work. Assigned topics often fall into this classification; the instructor knows that a particular work is an especially significant example of an important style and therefore directs the students to analyze that work and report their conclusions. A paper on a single work typically begins with a review of the background of the work and a summary of what has been written about the work in secondary sources. The main body of the paper is the student's analysis of the work, followed by a short conclusion and a bibliography.

Another type of topic is a comparative analysis; an example would be a comparison of early and late symphonies by Haydn. Analysis of similar works by different composers can be very instructive as well. A project that has worked well in classes on Renaissance music is a comparison of Dufay's *L'Homme armé* Mass with one of Josquin's Masses on the same *cantus firmus*. Because the source material, compositional process, and basic style are the same in the two works, the comparison isolates the differences in style between the two composers. If you are trying to design a comparative analysis project, it is important that the works be closely related stylistically. A study comparing a Schoenberg twelve-tone piece and a neoclassical work by Stravinsky would obviously show that the two works are fundamentally different—no great discovery. On the other hand, it would be interesting to compare twelve-tone works by Schoenberg and Webern, since that study would presumably uncover individual differences within the same basic style.

Sometimes it is useful to survey a larger group of related works in the same style. The danger is that the student may end up producing a list, dull to assemble and boring to read. That sort of project works only when such surveys do not exist already and the student has some personal reason to want to produce such a list, such as compiling a repertory of works useful for teaching.

Finally, there are biographical and historical studies that do not focus on analysis of specific works. Such projects might study, for example, a Renaissance court and its musical life, or the musical situation in turn-of-the-century Vienna. A biographical study of an important performer of the Baroque era, such as the *castrato* Farinelli or Gottfried Reiche, Bach's trumpeter at Leipzig, might enlighten the student about the importance of performers to the evolution of musical style, as well as the ways in which musical careers in that era differed from careers now. There are three potential problems connected with historical or biographical topics. First, all research ought to lead us to *music,* the art we are studying. Second, topics of this sort can sometimes result in summaries of material already readily available in standard sources, in which case they are pointless exercises. Third, students sometimes propose historical topics that are too broad-ranging. In classes in medieval music, for instance, students sometimes propose topics like the influence of Hebrew chant or Byzantine chant on Gregorian chant. Those are fascinating questions, but in order to deal adequately with such topics, one would need command of several languages, training in paleography, knowledge of several liturgical traditions and their historical development, access to liturgical manuscripts, and ten or twenty years of research. Obviously, those are not appropriate topics for a semester project.

You can now understand why professors assign specific topics, ask students to choose a topic from a prepared list, or insist on approving topics early in the semester. Some topics work, some do not, and some would take years to cover adequately. Trust your professor's judgment about topics; if you are really intent on pursuing an unusual topic, most instructors will try to help you to pursue that interest and still produce a successful paper.

WHAT RESEARCH MEANS

Since some students apparently do not know what the term *research* implies, we need to make a few things clear.

First of all, research is not just locating a group of relevant quotations and stringing them together in a paper, even if the writer includes quotation marks and appropriate footnotes. Reporting what authorities have said about a topic may be a useful way to begin a paper, but this step does not fulfill the researcher's responsibility. Research in any field must have a creative, personal side, especially in the arts, where we study the creations of human freedom and artistic vision. Even research in the natural sciences involves more than merely measuring and quantifying phenomena. It takes a creative mind to make the leap necessary to create a hypothesis to explain puzzling phenomena and the correct means to test this hypothesis. Research in the arts is not just gathering information, any more than musical analysis consists of listing and quantifying musical events. Facts of themselves are useless unless they lead to ideas. One must have a hypothesis and a conclusion. After the writer has quoted this authority and that authority, the reader wants to know what the writer thinks. Too often, students think their work is done if they have summarized what everyone else has written. A review of the literature may be useful or necessary, but true research involves much more than that.

Plagiarism. Stringing quotations together, adding the appropriate quotation marks and footnotes, does not constitute research. Stringing quotations together *without* quotation marks and footnotes is another question altogether. Some students are apparently not aware that copying uncredited quotations from books or articles, giving the impression that the copied words or paragraphs are the student's own words, constitutes plagiarism, a serious breach of academic ethics. In most colleges and universities, the standard response to a clear case of plagiarism is to treat the paper as unacceptable and to refer the case to a university committee on academic standards. Students sometimes claim that they were taught to write papers by copying uncredited quotations. Even if that were so, this practice is certainly not acceptable at the college level. In higher education, copying uncredited quotations is equivalent to cheating on the final examination and raises serious questions about whether the student should be allowed to continue pursuing a degree.

The sad thing about most cases of plagiarism is that they are so transparent. Generally, students resort to these tactics because writing is difficult for them. The act of plagiarism thus creates a strange hybrid paper; suddenly, in the midst of the student's own halting prose, the reader sees a paragraph in a completely different style, adorned with elegant metaphors, complex subjunctive constructions, and a vocabulary far beyond that of the student. Sometimes the student even copies archaic or foreign spellings— British spellings, like *honour* or *organise*, are a dead giveaway. I once saw *Durchfürung*, a German word used in nineteenth-century writings to denote what we now call "development," in the middle of a paragraph of flowery Victorian prose inserted in an otherwise poorly written paper. When I asked the student what the term meant, he had no idea. Perhaps some less obvious examples of plagiarism have escaped me, but generally, plagiarism is quite obvious. More important, it is universally regarded as a serious breach of scholarly ethics, with extremely serious consequences. No situation is desperate enough to justify risking one's college career. It would be much better to submit an honest paper and take the consequences than to try to pass off someone else's writing as your own work.

Research, then, involves more than stringing quotations together; that would be a book report, not a research paper. What should happen at some point is that all the information you have gathered, both from the secondary sources and from your analysis of the music, begins to coalesce around one central point, the main idea of your paper. The reader wants to know what you think. Do you agree with the secondary sources? Does your analysis of the music lead you to side with one opinion rather than another or to disagree with them all? Does your view of the work differ from the view reported in the standard literature?

Your hypothesis and conclusion need not be world-shaking. The reader of undergraduate papers does not expect to see conclusions like "This cantata could not possibly have been written by Bach," or "This Handel oratorio is actually based on a twelve-tone row." The reader does expect, however, to see your informed opinion, based on the research you have done. Too many papers stop abruptly after reporting on the secondary literature and the analysis process, as if the last page or two were inadvertently left out. As a scholar and musician, even as an apprentice in one or both fields, you have a responsibility to follow the research process to its conclusion, to risk taking a position, and to communicate your informed ideas and opinions about your topic.

GATHERING MATERIALS

Once you have a workable topic, the next step is to gather the materials you need. Start by assembling a bibliography on the topic. As you begin your search for information in the secondary sources, it is important to be thorough and systematic. Set aside a large block of time for this step, take notes on what you find, and keep your information in some organized fashion—either on separate cards, one card for each source, in a notebook, or in some other convenient way. Whatever system you use for gathering and storing information, it is important to be consistent and systematic. There is nothing worse than getting to the writing stage and finding that your notes are incomplete or no longer make sense to you. Each entry should include complete bibliographic information so that you do not have to return to each book to find out the date of publication, the page on which the material you want to quote appears, and other such details. The more complete and consistent your note-taking system is, the easier it will be to use the material when you get to the writing stage.

PLACES TO START

As you begin the search for information on your topic, start with the standard kinds of resources. The first thing to be aware of is that bibliographies on many topics have already been assembled and are published in several places. Obviously, starting with these existing bibliographies saves considerable time and effort and makes it less likely that you will overlook an important source. Lists of bibliographies appear in the guides for graduate students; here are some basic resources, with some advice on how to use them.

Dictionaries and Encyclopedias

The standard way to start a research project is to consult musical dictionaries and encyclopedias. The following are some of the standard musical reference works.

APEL, WILLI, ed. *The Harvard Dictionary of Music.* Third edition. Cambridge, Mass.: Belknap, 1969.
BLUME, FRIEDRICH, ed. *Die Musik in Geschichte und Gegenwart.* Kassel: Bärenreiter, 1949–1979.
SADIE, STANLEY, ed. *The New Grove Dictionary of Music and Musicians.* London: Macmillan, 1980.
SLONIMSKY, NICOLAS, ed. *Baker's Biographical Dictionary of Musicians.* Seventh edition. New York: Schirmer, 1984.

Baker's Biographical Dictionary is a one-volume biographical dictionary, listing composers, performers, and theorists; worklists and selective bibliographies are included. The *Harvard Dictionary* is a one-volume dictionary of terms, with some longer articles and useful selective bibliographies. These two volumes constitute a basic reference library; students should consider owning their own copies.

The *New Grove,* as it is called, is the most important encyclopedia of music and is the best place to start for bibliographical information. Each article was written by an expert in that particular field. Some of the articles are book-length, and all contain complete worklists and bibliographies that were up-to-date at the time of publication. All music libraries have this basic resource on their reference shelves; it can be found in many public libraries as well. Always check the *New Grove* and use some imagination as you search for information; the material you seek might be found in an article on a composer or in articles on genres, instruments, terms, or historical eras.

The German encyclopedia, known familiarly as MGG, was the basic resource until recently; now it has been largely supplanted by the *New Grove.* It is still useful for its articles by recognized experts and for its bibliographies. All the articles are signed.

There are other specialized dictionaries and encyclopedias; see the Duckles bibliography for details. The four publications listed above are the basic resources, and the *New Grove* is by far the most helpful.

Note that there are supplementary *New Grove* dictionaries dealing with instruments and American music.

HITCHCOCK, H. WILEY, and STANLEY SADIE, eds. *The New Grove Dictionary of American Music.* Four volumes. London: Macmillan, 1986.

SADIE, STANLEY, ed. *The New Grove Dictionary of Musical Instruments.* Three volumes. London: Macmillan, 1980.

Histories of Music

Most histories of music include bibliographical notes, either at the end of each chapter or in the back of the book. These bibliographies are another good place to start, once you locate the chapter in the book or series that includes the area you are researching. The following are the standard one-volume histories.

CROCKER, RICHARD L. *A History of Musical Style.* New York: McGraw-Hill, 1966. Reprint, Dover, 1986. The bibliography, entitled "Selected Study Materials" and organized by chapters, begins on page 538.

GROUT, DONALD J., and CLAUDE V. PALISCA. *A History of Western Music.* Fourth edition. New York: W. W. Norton & Co., 1988. Bibliographies appear at the end of each chapter.

ROSENSTIEL, LEONIE, general editor. *Schirmer History of Music.* New York: Schirmer, 1982. Bibliographies appear at the end of each chapter.

The multivolume histories of music also contain useful selective bibliographies. Among the standard music history series are the following publications.

The New Oxford History of Music, ed. Anselm Hughes and Gerald Abraham. A series of eleven volumes, containing articles by recognized experts; each article contains a bibliography.

The Norton Introduction to Music History. Two volumes, *Medieval Music* by Richard Hoppin and *Romantic Music* by Leon Plantinga, have appeared so far. Each of the six volumes will contain extensive bibliographies, organized by chapter and located in the back of the book.

Prentice-Hall History of Music Series, H. Wiley Hitchcock, general editor. Six volumes on Western music, one on American music, and four on musics of other cultures, each with bibliographical notes at the end of each chapter.

You should also check to see if there is a specialized history of the genre you are working with, like Newman's multivolume history of the sonata, Einstein's three-volume history of the Italian madrigal, and similar studies.

Biographies

If someone has written a biography of the composer you are studying, it may be very helpful for your project, particularly if it is a "life and works," including description and analysis of the composer's works. Biographies are classified in the Library of Congress system under the number ML (for "Music Literature") 410; within that section, books are shelved alphabetically by composer, so that one can browse for biographies by looking under the composer's name. In the Dewey Decimal System, all biographies are shelved together under the classification 92 (shorthand for 920), then alphabetically by subject. Thus biographies of composers are located with all the other biographies. Unfortunately, not all biographies are serious research studies; later in this chapter, we will discuss the researcher's responsibility to evaluate sources and use them carefully. Still, biographies are an important resource for research.

Thematic Catalogs

If a composer's works have been listed in a thematic catalog or *Verzeichnis*, the researcher may find such a catalog very helpful. The most famous examples of thematic catalogs are the Köchel catalog of the works of Mozart, which is organized chronologically, and Schmieder's *Bach-Werke-Verzeichnis*, organized by genre. These are only the best-known examples; a random sampling of composers whose works have been systematically cataloged includes Beethoven, Brahms, Haydn, Lully, Schubert, Schoenberg, Shostakovich, Strauss, Stravinsky, and Vivaldi. A complete list of thematic catalogs may be found in Barry S. Brook, *Thematic Catalogues in Music: An Annotated Bibliography* (Hillsdale, N.Y.: Pendragon Press, 1972). One advantage of these resources is that the entry for each work often includes a bibliography *on that specific work*. In the Bach catalog, for instance, the entry for each cantata lists articles on that particular cantata and lists the pages in general books where that work is discussed. Obviously, the efficient researcher will want to take advantage of these resources.

Articles

An enormous body of recent research is found only in musicological journals, such as *The Journal of the American Musicological Society, Musical Quarterly, Acta Musicologica, Music Review*, and similar scholarly publications. Many students ignore this important resource or do not know how to find journal articles relevant to their topics. Articles are the only source of substantial information on some topics; one often finds that the standard secondary sources have little to say on many topics. The best way to acquaint yourself with the journals and get some idea of the sort of research they publish is to browse through the current issues of periodicals in the music library.

Locating articles among the scores of scholarly journals may seem an intimidating task for the neophyte researcher. There are resources designed to help researchers locate articles on specific topics. Many journals publish cumulative listings of the articles they have published. There are also two general guides that list articles published in the musical journals. The first is the *Music Index*, a listing of articles published in selected music periodicals. The *Music Index* began publication in 1949; it is published monthly, and cumulative listings are published annually. The quickest way to locate articles is to first search through the annual cumulative listings and then consult the monthly issues for their more detailed listings of the articles that look promising. It takes time to go through all the annual listings, but it is an excellent way to locate articles related to your topic.

Another important resource is the *International Inventory of Music Literature*, known as RILM from the initials of its title in French. This index lists books, articles, dissertations, and other publications, and is published several times a year. Cumulative listings are published every five years. Using RILM can save considerable time because of the inclusiveness of its coverage. Articles in collections that are not regularly indexed or included in card catalogs are indexed in RILM; it can be very helpful indeed.

If you have not used these resources, it would be helpful to spend some time browsing in them, so that when you need to use them for a research project you will have some familiarity with them. Pick a topic like *The St. Matthew Passion*, or Mahler's *Kindertotenlieder*, and see what you can find in each of the resources listed above. Comparing the coverage in these various publications will give you a good idea of the particular advantages of each.

Dissertations

Doctoral dissertations can be very helpful to the researcher, since they should contain information based on primary resources and complete bibliographies. Reference libraries contain published lists of dissertations accepted in American and European libraries and abstracts of dissertations published by University Microfilms of Ann Arbor. Music libraries frequently order copies of dissertations, and anyone can order a copy of any dissertation from University Microfilms. If you find a listing of a dissertation you would like to consult but are worried about the cost or getting a copy in time, talk to your professor; he or she might want the library to order a copy.

EVALUATING RESOURCES

It is important for the researcher to realize that he or she must exercise critical judgment when consulting any published materials. Not everything in print is to be taken as gospel truth or followed blindly. Not all biographies, for example, are scholarly studies. Biographies run the gamut from definitive studies, like Robbins Landon's multivolume study of Haydn's life and works, to overromanticized nineteenth-century biographies, which may be entertaining but are not very helpful for scholarly work. One quickly gets a sense of how scholarly a biography is. If one has to choose between two biographies, the more recent one or the one that shows evidence of serious scholarly research is more to be trusted than the earlier or more popular treatment. The same comparison can be made about other kinds of resources; there are different kinds of journals, different sorts of histories, even different levels of reference works intended for different audiences.

The researcher often finds that information, right or wrong, is repeated unchallenged from secondary source to secondary source. You are free—in fact, obliged—to take issue with assumptions found in print if your research indicates that those assumptions are not borne out by the facts or by careful analysis of the music. That is precisely what the researcher's task is—to raise questions about what is written in secondary sources. Sources are not to be followed blindly but are to be judged realistically and critically. A one-volume history of music, for example, cannot be expected to include up-to-date reports of research findings in all areas or the latest information about every composer mentioned; that is not its purpose. On the other hand, one cannot expect a narrowly focused scholarly article to provide the broad view one expects to find in a one-volume history. Evaluation of sources is one of the major responsibilities of the researcher.

FOREIGN-LANGUAGE SOURCES

The responsible researcher cannot ignore important books and articles just because they happen to be written in a language other than English. It is a fact of scholarly life that many important books and articles are written in German, Latin, French, Italian, and other languages. German, French, and English are the standard languages in which research in all fields is published. If you do not read German and a German biography or article appears to be an important source for your topic, then ask someone reliable to translate the relevant sections for you. There are people on any college campus who can read any language under the sun. Bear in mind, also, that tables and bibliographies are exactly the same in German sources as in English ones. Students sometimes avoid using the Schmieder catalog of Bach's works because "it's in German." The book can be useful to anyone, regardless of language experience.

SCORES AND RECORDINGS

The researcher needs to apply the same sort of critical judgment to scores and recordings that he or she applies to books and articles. There are different kinds of scores. Primary sources—manuscripts and original editions—are the most reliable but the most difficult to find, and may be difficult for a nonspecialist to read. Scholarly editions attempt to present an edition of the music that represents as exactly as possible what the composer actually wrote, based on surviving autograph materials and the earliest possible printed editions. Then there are performing scores, some of them quite reliable and others heavily edited. The question of editions is most critical with early music. For example, the old performing editions of Bach's keyboard works, edited by Busoni and others, are cluttered with fingerings, slurs, dynamic markings, and other editorial additions that have nothing to do with what Bach actually wrote. Obviously, scholarly work should not be based on these heavily edited editions, but on the *Urtext*, a clean scholarly edition that tries to duplicate what the composer wrote. It is better to find a reliable scholarly edition in the collected sets or collected works of a composer, and make a photocopy of that score to use as your working copy, than it is to base your work on a more accessible performing edition that may or may not faithfully represent what the composer wrote. Browse through the M1, M2, and M3 sections of the music library to get some sense of the wealth of scholarly editions available to you. Note that some collections are organized by countries or genres; the M3 section contains the collected works of individual composers. The Dewey Decimal System groups these editions similarly and has special numbers for each type of collection. There are two standard guides to collected sets found in the reference sections of most music libraries.

CHARLES, SYDNEY ROBINSON. *A Handbook of Music and Music Literature in Sets and Series.* New York: The Free Press, 1972.
HEYER, ANNA HARRIET. *Historical Sets, Collected Editions, and Monuments of Music: A Guide to Their Contents.* Third edition; two volumes. Chicago: American Library Association, 1980.

The same critical judgment must be applied to recordings, particularly to recordings of early music. Although we know much more about authentic performance than we did some years ago, many questions of performance practice are still hotly contested issues, and we have no final answers. Still, if you have a choice of recordings to use for your project, it makes sense to use one that takes historical authenticity as one of its goals. Check the record jacket to see whether old instruments are used, how the edition was arrived at, and whether the performing group specializes in old music.

Critical judgment should be applied not only to the recorded performance but also to the liner notes. Sometimes liner notes are written by well-known experts and based on serious historical study. At other times, the space is devoted to biographies of the performers or advertisements for other recordings, with a paragraph or two left for discussion of the music. Serious liner notes, especially those signed by a known expert, or booklets included with multidisc albums are appropriate to cite in a paper. Brief, unsigned comments are not likely to provide the sort of material that you would want to cite.

WHEN TO STOP: HOW MUCH RESEARCH IS ENOUGH?

The point at which one decides that one has gathered enough information for a paper will vary, depending on the topic and the limits set by the instructor when the paper was assigned. Usually, undergraduates are not expected to assemble bibliographies of the size and depth one expects to see in a master's thesis or a graduate paper.

There are two extremes to be avoided. Some students are satisfied with a citation or two from their music history textbooks, the same all-purpose encyclopedias they used for their high school papers, or popular books with titles like *The Wonderful World of Music*. In other words, some students gather their information from the wrong kind of resources and never approach serious research. Others find their card files bulging with citations and keep uncovering new resources that they feel obliged to include. If the research phase seems to be getting out of control, especially if the information you find seems not to support your preliminary hypothesis, it may be time to arrange a conference with your instructor. It may be necessary to agree on some limits to your research, or you may be approaching your research in the wrong way. It is also possible that your topic is too broad and needs some rethinking. It is probably helpful at that point to step back a bit from your research to see it in perspective and to decide whether what you have done is appropriate for the project.

What should happen near the end of the research phase is that all the information begins to fall into place in your mind, to lead to clear ideas and opinions, and to coalesce into a logical, coherent framework. The mass of information has to be shaped by you into a coherent plan. In the interests of unity and coherence, you may not be able to use every item you have uncovered in your research; one usually does more research than one can actually use. The next step is to organize everything you have discovered in the research phase into a logical outline, with one central idea or hypothesis, evidence in support of the central idea gathered from secondary sources and from your analysis of the music, and a conclusion. Thoughtful and diligent research is critical, but it is only the first phase. A mass of information is not a paper but raw material that must be organized into a clear and coherent presentation.

chapter 4

Writing a Research Paper

This chapter describes the process of writing a research paper, step by step, after the research phase is completed. Naturally, the writing process will vary, depending on the specific topic and focus of the paper; this chapter will discuss general principles and practical advice applicable to most papers.

THE OUTLINE

The first step in writing the paper is to design a clear outline, so that when you begin to write, you will know exactly where you are going, what comes next, and what material belongs where. This is the point at which you must make the difficult decisions about what to include and what to leave out and how the material should be ordered. The outlining stage is critical and has at least as much impact on the quality of the eventual paper as any other step. It is in the process of outlining that you settle the critical questions of unity, coherence, and logical flow. Once you create a clear and logical outline, writing the paper becomes a matter of putting flesh on the outline's skeleton. If your outline is a jumbled, incoherent mess, your paper will also be a mess. Usually, the outline will include an introduction, the main body of the paper, and a conclusion.

Introduction

The function of an introduction is to ease into your topic, put it in some perspective, and announce the main point of your paper. Read through some articles in one of the musicological journals to see how introductions work. They often start with a general idea and then move to the specific topic and point of the paper.

There are two extremes to be avoided in introductions. The first is the abrupt start, which plunges directly into the body of the paper, disorienting the unwary reader. Suppose a paper were to begin like this: "In the first measure, we can already see the materials on which the entire movement will be based." The reader thinks, "Wait a minute. What period are we talking about? Which composer? Which work? Which movement?" The fact that the paper has a title page announcing the topic does not free the writer from the obligation to lead the reader gently into the topic. An introduction should introduce the general topic, the specific area the paper will deal with, and the precise point the paper will try to establish.

The other extreme is the long introduction that develops a life of its own and becomes a separate paper, bringing up issues that are not germane to the main point of the paper and wandering away from the topic instead of leading the reader into it. Books on writing recommend as a general rule that an introduction should occupy no more than one-tenth of the paper's length. An introduction may need to be longer, if, for example, it is necessary to define terms or concepts that are important to the following discussion. Generally, if the introduction to your fifteen-page paper runs beyond two or three pages, you need to find and excise the extraneous material.

The introduction should include a clear idea of where the paper is going and announce the main point that you will try to establish. At the outline stage, you need to decide exactly how you will introduce your topic and what you should and should not include in your introduction.

Body

Next, you need to outline the main points of the body of your paper, including all the subtopics that will be included in each of the main points. It is a good idea to work out your outline in considerable detail, even to the level of individual paragraphs, so that when you begin writing, you know exactly what goes where and what comes next. It is at this point that you need to make the decisions about the order in which the material will be presented. You should also include in your outline some idea of the methodology to be followed in establishing each point—where musical examples will be most effective, where quotations from the secondary sources are appropriate, which points depend on analysis, and so forth. You should end with an outline so specific that if you were to submit the outline alone, your instructor would have a clear idea of what you intend to accomplish. The more time you spend fussing with the outline, the more logical, coherent, and convincing your paper will be.

Conclusion

Often, the most difficult section of a paper to write is the conclusion. The writer feels that everything has been said already and does not want to repeat what the paper has already explained. Conclusions are necessary, however, not only to reemphasize your main point, but also to wrap up the study in a tidy, memorable way. You can connect your main idea with the existing body of research on your topic, show what your research adds to critical opinion of the composer in question, or point to other areas in which similar research would be appropriate. Be careful not to go overboard in your conclusion. At this point, some students, probably relieved to find themselves near the end of the paper, get carried away and lapse into flowery or exaggerated language about the world-shaking importance of this particular topic. Provide a logical and forceful closure for the reader, then stop.

Revising the Outline

Once you have a tentative outline, stop and take a critical look at it. The problems pointed out by the committees that read theses and dissertations are almost always *outline* problems. Material is discussed in the wrong place, the order is not logical, the emphasis is wrong, some material does not fit with the main point of the project, or necessary material is left out. *It is much easier to modify the design and order of your paper at the outline stage than it is at the later stages of the draft or final copy.* Check the outline carefully for unity, coherence, and logical flow. Experiment with a different order within the body of your paper. Would your main point be more convincing if the order of supporting arguments were changed? Is the last argument the weakest or the strongest? Is there a weak argument that might better be left out? Is there anything in the outline that is not related to your main point and therefore belongs in some other paper? Is there a subject that is discussed in several different places, and would it make more sense to combine those discussions in one place? Tinker with your outline, try a different order, experiment. The more logical, coherent, and forceful your outline is, the more logical and convincing the paper will be. The time you devote to revising your outline will pay off in a stronger and more effective paper.

WRITING THE DRAFT

After you have designed an outline that works, with everything in its proper place, the next step is to sit down, face the blank paper or screen, and start writing what you want to say. The important thing is to get it all out, even in less than perfect form, to see how the first version turns out. Since you have allowed time for editing, your concern at the draft stage should be to get something down on paper, imperfect or not, so that you have something to polish and edit later. If you have trouble getting started with the introduction, begin with the body of the paper, and return later to write the introduction. The important thing is to complete a draft. The most efficient way to draft a paper, provided that you can compose at a keyboard, is to use word-processing equipment; in the following chapter, we will discuss the advantages of using word-processing equipment, as well as some potential problems you should be aware of. The main thing to bear in mind as you write the draft is that it is only a draft, not the final version you will submit. Changes can always be made at a later stage. You cannot edit or revise until you have completed the draft. The draft is the raw material that you will refine and polish to produce the final paper.

Musical Examples

While you are writing the draft, or even earlier in the outline stage, you should decide whether musical examples are necessary or appropriate to your paper and how you will deal with them.

In papers whose focus is analytical, it is usually helpful to include musical examples; a carefully chosen musical example may be more effective than several pages of descriptive prose. If you are trying to make a point about an unusual cadence, for example, *show* the reader the cadence, along with your explanation. It usually is not necessary to include the entire score with your paper; carefully selected examples, however, can be very helpful to the reader.

There are several ways to include musical examples in your paper. You can write out your own examples, particularly if you are an experienced copyist. You can also photocopy the particular measures or sections of a score that will make your point more clear. Always consider clarity first; the examples should clearly support your point, not confuse the reader. Oversize Romantic orchestral scores, for instance, not only are difficult to photocopy, but also may be confusing or distracting to your reader. A reduced score in your own hand might be clearer. If you use photocopied examples, be sure that they are complete. You may need to add clefs if the measures you copy do not include them. If musical examples, either hand copied or photocopied, are to be included in the paper, the final versions of the examples have to be prepared before the final typing of the paper so that whoever types the paper can leave sufficient space for each example. One must also be sure that examples are firmly attached to the page with double-stick tape or some other means. Another strategy is to photocopy the finished paper, keep the original, and submit the copy; the examples in the photocopy are permanently fixed on the page.

Sometimes the best way to illustrate the point you are making is to add your analytic markings to a photocopy of the score. Some students have a talent for graphics and can mark a score in such a way that the reader immediately sees the point that the writer is trying to make. Others submit marked scores that are as confusing as a Beethoven sketch, with the point of the example obscured by sloppy or unclear markings. One cannot rely on a marked score alone to make one's point about the design of a work; there must always be some verbal explanation as well. One final point: Whenever you include musical examples, whether they appear in the text or in an appendix, each example must be clearly captioned so that the reader knows not only exactly what the example represents—the specific work, movement, and measure numbers—but also precisely where the example fits into the text.

Diagrams, Graphics, and Tables

Related to the question of musical examples is the question of designing your own diagrams or graphic representations of musical events. Particularly in questions of overall structure, diagrams can be extremely useful, provided that they are clear and make the point effectively. One can diagram the structure of the first movement of Bach's Brandenburg Concerto No. 5, for example, on a single page, whereas the *Bach-Gesellschaft* edition of the score occupies twenty-two pages. A table might be an effective way to show how the *cantus firmus* is used in the various movements of a Renaissance Mass. A diagram might be the best way to depict the loose or unusual structures sometimes found in Romantic symphonic works. The point is always *effectiveness*—will this diagram or graphic analysis be clear to the reader? Is it the best way to make the point I am trying to make? Does it make sense, or does it need further modification to be clear? You can always test the clarity of a diagram by showing it to a fellow student. If it makes its point clearly, it helps the paper enormously; if it does not, tear it up—it will only detract from the effectiveness of your paper.

Footnotes

While you are writing the draft, you need to decide where footnotes are needed, put the footnote numbers in your text, and write the footnotes as you write the text, so that everything matches up correctly. There is nothing worse at the stage of final typing than seeing a footnote number in the text and finding no footnote to go with that number. In this matter, as well as in most matters connected with writing a paper, the key is to be precise and systematic early in the process. We will deal with details of footnote format, along with other format issues, in Chapter 6. Here we will discuss two fundamental questions concerning footnotes: when to include them and where they should be placed in the finished paper.

Once you understand the purpose of footnotes, the rules about them make perfect sense. Footnotes are included in a paper in order to establish that the writer has some basis for the assertions he or she makes and so that the writer can acknowledge his or her indebtedness to outside sources of information. The idea is that the readers, if they wish, can go to the sources to check the information themselves or to pursue other lines of investigation. There are two extremes to be avoided. Some students include very few footnotes, even when they are obviously repeating information they discovered in their research. Others footnote nearly every sentence, a practice that is both tiresome and unnecessary. Some general guidelines may help students to deal with this question.

First, every direct or indirect quotation must have a footnote. If you quote someone directly—that is, copying the quotation word for word, with quotation marks—you must also include a footnote that tells exactly where that quotation appears. If you cite someone's opinion indirectly, without quoting that person's exact words, you still need a footnote to back up your claim that the person actually said what you ascribe to him or her. The following sentence is an example of indirect quotation.

Stuckenschmidt claims that Schoenberg first conceived the idea for *Pierrot Lunaire* in 1910, whereas Rufer cites the composer's letter to Berg in 1912 as the first indication that he intended to set these poems.

The writer cannot claim that the authors made those statements without a footnote listing the exact places in the writings of Stuckenschmidt and Rufer where those assertions are made. The footnote must list the books or articles, including the necessary information about place and date of publication, as well as the pages on which the statements can be found.

Second, footnotes are not needed to support statements that are common knowledge. This rule can be slippery—how does one determine what is "common knowledge"? At the extremes, the answer is fairly obvious.

Beethoven composed nine symphonies.
J. S. Bach died in 1750, after a long and productive career.

Those sentences hardly need footnotes. On the other hand, consider this sentence:

It is not historically authentic to perform the Beethoven sonatas on an English fortepiano, since Beethoven preferred the pianos made in Vienna.

Here you certainly need a footnote. The reader wants to know how you know what Beethoven thought and where you found that information. In between these extremes, one must use one's judgment about the common knowledge issue. It is helpful to keep in mind the audience for whom the paper is intended. Rather than trying to guess at what your instructor might consider common knowledge, imagine yourself reading your paper to the other members of your class. What is general knowledge to a group of music majors in a music history class is different from general knowledge among the population at large. Do not footnote what would be obvious to your colleagues. When in doubt, err on the side of too many footnotes rather than too few.

One helpful way to avoid obtrusive numbers of footnotes is to use one general footnote for a *section* of a paper rather than attaching a footnote to each sentence. If your paper includes a biographical sketch of a composer, for example, it is not necessary to include a separate footnote to support each item of information—date of birth, education, positions, important works, and date of death. You can include a single footnote early in that section, referring the reader to the sources where this biographical information may be found. If an analytical section makes use of published analyses, you might list them in a single note at the beginning of the section and thereafter footnote only direct or indirect quotations. The best way to get a sense of proper footnote use is to read articles in scholarly journals; the scholars who write them and the editors who approve them understand correct footnote practice. Note as you skim through articles that the footnotes tend to cluster at the beginning of the article, where the author lists other publications that have dealt with this topic and the primary materials on which his or her research is based. Footnotes appear less frequently after the first few pages, as the author moves into the discussion of his or her own findings.

A final question has to do with where the footnotes should be placed in the final paper. The rules for theses and dissertations used to require that the footnotes be placed, as the name indicates, at the bottom of the page. One practical reason for that requirement is that dissertations often circulate in microfilm form, making it inconvenient to scroll through the entire paper to find each footnote. Another system is to place the notes at the end of each chapter, or all together at the end of the text, before the bibliography. This system of "endnotes" rather than "footnotes" is usually acceptable for undergraduate papers. You should check to be sure that this system is acceptable to your instructor before submitting a paper with endnotes; the instructor might want the students to follow the more formal footnote system.

The central issue about footnotes is the writer's responsibility to acknowledge his or her sources and back up his or her claims. Once you understand the purpose of footnotes, the questions about when to footnote and when not to footnote usually solve themselves; in doubtful cases, ask your instructor.

Bibliography

The last section of your draft is the bibliography. Questions of bibliography format will be discussed, along with other format issues, in Chapter 6. At this point, we need to discuss what should and should not be included in your bibliography, a question that seems to puzzle many students.

There are different points of view on the question of what should be included in a bibliography. The strictest position is that nothing should be listed in the bibliography that was not actually cited in the paper. In other words, only those publications that appear in the footnotes should be listed in the bibliography. A less strict position would allow those publications actually consulted by the writer to be included in the bibliography, whether or not they are cited in the footnotes. The most inclusive position would allow the writer to include any sources he has run across, whether or not he has actually consulted them all.

A related issue has to do with secondhand references—if you cannot get your hands on book A, which is obviously an important source, but it is quoted in book B, which you *did* consult, is it ethical to list both book B and book A in your bibliography? If you feel uncomfortable listing a publication that you think belongs in your bibliography but that you have not seen, one solution is to list it and then add a note such as "not available for this study." That way, the reader knows that you are aware of the existence of an important source, but you cannot be accused of creating the false impression that you have actually used the book.

In regard to the other issues of limiting the bibliography to materials you have quoted or actually seen, check to see what your instructor's policy is. If one goal of the project is practice in research techniques and assembling a bibliography, the instructor might want the students to include as many items as they can, whether or not they have actually consulted them.

One last reminder: I pointed out earlier that it is a mistake to pad a bibliography with silly items just to make it look longer. You should omit reference to the general works that you used for reports in high school, like the *Encyclopedia Americana*, or books that are written for record collectors or junior high students rather than university-level students. Do not include your music history textbook—the whole point of research is to go beyond the readily available sources of information and to question everything that you read, even in scholarly publications.

Finally, the instructor may ask you to *annotate* your bibliography, which means to include brief critical comments on each item. Helpful annotations point out the special advantages or limits of each publication. Comments like "the definitive biography, based on newly discovered primary sources," or "particularly useful for the analyses of major works" not only show that you are a critical, intelligent reader, but also provide useful information for the reader who may want to pursue related research questions in those same sources. Annotated bibliographies are standard assignments in some graduate courses, but they may also be required at the undergraduate level, and students should know what the term implies.

EDITING AND REVISING THE DRAFT

Let us assume that you now have before you a handwritten or typewritten draft of your complete paper. The draft is an early stage of the paper, not the finished product you will hand in—it is raw material and needs considerable editing, revising, and polishing before you have a finished paper. Allow a large block of time for editing and revising; it sometimes takes as long to edit and polish as it did to produce the draft, particularly if you are one of those people who write drafts quickly. It is also helpful to let the draft "cool off" several times—that is, to pause between editing sessions. When you return to a draft after letting it sit for a while, it is easier to see the mistakes and awkward phrases that need revising. Somehow you can be more objective about your creation when you return to it after a pause of a day or two. The sentence that seemed to have an eloquent ring as you drafted it, perhaps late at night, may look childish or pretentious a few days later.

As you edit your draft, you need to assume a different mental stance from the one you took when you were creating the draft. At this point, you must try to be a critical reader, questioning every word, every phrase, prepared to shuffle paragraphs or sections if moving them will make your paper more effective, prepared to throw sentences or paragraphs out altogether if they do not work, even ready to tear up the whole draft and start again if necessary. It is much better for you to discover your own bad writing than it is to see it circled in red when the paper is returned to you.

When you are editing your draft, you need to work on several different levels. You may need to read through the draft several times, criticizing it from a different point of view each time. One reading should concentrate on unity and coherence, viewing the entire paper as a unit, questioning the order and effectiveness of your arguments. Have you said exactly what you wanted to say or does your prose talk around the central issues, without ever actually getting to the point? Are topics in the proper order or does the draft ramble? Do you keep returning to matters you have already discussed? Suppose you change the order of arguments or paragraphs—would a different order be more effective? Are there abrupt transitions? Do you perhaps need to add some material to make clear that you are shifting to a new subject or approach? Try to approach your work as a critical reader. Can you follow the train of thought as it is laid out in the draft? Are there gaps in the logical argument, assumptions that are never clearly explained? Do you know at all times where you are in the argument? Is it clear where each section fits in the overall progress of the argument?

To deal with these questions, you need to view the paper as a unit. You may need to ignore details of wording and writing style for the moment. If you plunge immediately into revising at the level of detail, it may be difficult to keep the large picture in your mind. Checking for unity and coherence should be done early in the editing process, since it is a waste of time to polish the wording of a paragraph if you will need to eliminate it later for reasons of unity and coherence. Be sure that material will survive as part of the final paper before you polish it.

You also need to criticize and revise your draft at the level of detail, asking yourself whether this word, this phrase, this sentence says what you want to say or whether you need to cross it out and try another way. Mark the cases of weak wording, the awkward phrases, the sentences whose syntax is jumbled and unclear, and the paragraphs that may need to be completely rewritten, and then try to solve each of those problems. It may take several evenings of hard work to polish the draft to the point where you feel confident that your words say exactly what you want to say, with the clarity and emphasis you intended.

At some point, you might want to read the paper aloud to yourself. Mistakes—particularly pretentious or flowery language and jumbled syntax—become obvious when you read your prose aloud. It is true that written style and spoken style are two different things, but if you find it difficult to read one of your own sentences in a way that makes sense, it probably needs some reworking. Jumbled syntax usually means that the thought is jumbled. When you run into a tangled and confusing sentence in your draft, back up and think again about exactly what you are trying to say and how to say it more clearly and effectively.

Chapters 11–14 will discuss some principles of effective writing, with examples of how to go about improving your wording and sentence structure. Our concern here is not with the nuts and bolts of editing, but with understanding the importance of this step and the necessity to work hard at the process of cutting, revising, and polishing your paper. *Nobody writes perfect drafts.* The quality of your finished paper will depend to a great extent on the amount of work you put into this essential step. Brilliant ideas do not turn themselves into effective papers; in fact, unless you communicate your ideas clearly and effectively, no one will ever know that they are brilliant.

Leave enough time for the editing stage so that you can revise, wait a day or two, then return and revise again. The more effort you put into the editing stage, the better your paper will be. Without extensive editing, your paper stands little or no chance of being successful.

THE CLEAN COPY

By now, assuming you began with a typed or handwritten draft, you have a sheaf of marked-up papers, with arrows pointing to revised versions or new paragraphs to insert at various points. Sentences and paragraphs have been crossed out, moved around, and reassembled. The next stage is to produce a clean typed copy. The best way to do this is to type the final copy yourself; it is asking a lot of a friend to expect him or her to work through your marked-up draft. Besides, unless your typist is a music major, how can you expect him or her to understand what you are talking about, let alone know the correct spelling of technical terms? If you are going to type the paper yourself, allow sufficient time for this step. Typing a paper always takes longer than one expects, and it is difficult to maintain concentration for long periods. The longer you continue typing at one sitting, the more mistakes creep in. Words and lines of copy are left out, misspellings start to multiply, and the end result is not what you had in mind. It is much better to have the leisure to do this step carefully and attentively.

PROOFREADING

Whether your final copy is typed by you or a friend, or printed with the aid of word-processing equipment, the writing process is still not complete when the final copy is in your hand. There is one more important step—proofreading. There is no justification for assuming that everything is perfect in your typed copy. In fact, if you or someone else typed it in the wee hours of the morning, under pressure to meet an onrushing deadline, you can assume that the copy will include typographical errors that need correcting. It is hard to understand why students skip this final stage, when they have already spent so much time on research, writing, and editing. The actual proofreading does not take very long; correcting the mistakes you find may take more time. Errors can be covered with white-out; corrections can be made in black pen on your final copy unless they are extensive or several words have been left out. In that case, you may need to retype a page or two; there is a limit to the number of handwritten corrections one can make and still have the paper look like a careful, professional piece of work. You may also need to add accents, umlauts, and diacritical marks to foreign words in your text or footnotes. At this point, you need to paste in the musical examples, and you should make a final check to see that all the examples are in their proper places and clearly captioned.

The necessity of proofreading has always seemed obvious to me, but students frequently skip this final step. Remember that proofreading is the *writer's* responsibility; if the paper is unacceptable because it is a sloppy, unprofessional piece of work and no one bothered to proofread it, the low grade goes to the writer, not to the friend who typed it. Pride in your work necessitates careful attention to this final step.

After proofreading, correcting whatever errors have crept into the typed version of the paper, adding accents, and pasting in musical examples, *then* you finally have a paper ready to submit. A paper prepared with this kind of care will represent your best work, communicate your ideas as clearly and effectively as possible, and show that you are a competent researcher, capable of producing professional-quality work.

KEEP A COPY

Assuming you have worked carefully through each of the steps of producing a first-class paper, as explained in this chapter, there is still one more thing you should do before submitting the paper. It is a good idea to take the paper to a copy center and have a copy made. There are several reasons for this step. Professors seldom lose papers, but some professors have been known not to return papers or to take an inordinately long time to return them. Even if the papers are returned promptly, they may be covered with corrections and comments. Either way, it is good for you to have a clean copy of the paper for your files. You might need to submit examples of your work if you apply for admission to graduate school. If the copy you hand in comes back with a paragraph of glowing praise on the title page, you can always submit that copy to the graduate school. Even if graduate school is not in your plans at the moment, it still makes sense to save copies of the papers that represent your best work.

There are other advantages to making a copy of your paper. If it is agreeable to your instructor, you may want to hand in the photocopy and keep the original for your files. Many of the imperfections visible in the original, such as corrections or imperfectly drawn accent marks or umlauts, are masked by the photocopying process. More important, pasted-in musical examples become part of the page, differences in color between the typing paper and the music paper on which the examples are copied wash out in the copy, and the copy you submit shows less evidence of the process of putting it together.

CONCLUSION

The process of writing a paper the right way is long, involved, and time-consuming, a far cry from the desperate scramble during the last week before the deadline, or the two or three long nights' work that some students think is sufficient to produce a decent paper. The process outlined in this chapter occupies several weeks, if one includes the research phase. Even the process of writing the draft, editing, final typing, and proofreading takes more than a few evenings' work. Remember that no one writes perfect drafts. The quality of the paper you turn in is in direct proportion to the amount of time and effort you put into producing it. Provided that you have done adequate research and have thought carefully about the topic, your paper will succeed or fail as a direct result of the time and care you expend to see that your finished product meets accepted academic standards.

chapter 5

Using a Word Processor to Produce a Paper

Many students now use word-processing equipment to produce their research papers; many colleges and universities provide terminals and printers for the use of students. This modern technology can make the process of writing and editing a paper, as described in Chapter 4, much more efficient. Unfortunately, the advent of the computer has not noticeably improved the quality of student writing. Word-processing equipment speeds up the production of shoddy papers just as readily as it facilitates careful writing and editing. Assuming that more and more students will produce their papers in this way, we need to consider some of the advantages of word processors, as well as some limitations that students should be aware of. Some of these comments will undoubtedly be too elementary for students who are experienced users of this equipment, but they may be useful for less experienced users. It is not the place of this book to discuss specific brands of hardware or specific word-processing programs. Our focus here is on the general issues raised by the widespread use of this new technology.

ADVANTAGES OF WORD PROCESSING

Anyone who has written papers both ways—on a typewriter and on a word processor—much prefers the second way. It is hard to believe that we ever managed to write anything without a word processor. The main advantage of word-processing equipment, of course, is that it saves time and eliminates repetitive tasks. You can draft and edit on the screen; once the text is exactly the way you want it, pushing a few buttons produces the printed paper. Since you never have to retype the paper, you avoid the risk of introducing a new generation of typographical errors with each retyping. You can draft like the wind, confident that you can return again and again to polish the draft. You can edit extensively, cutting and adding, moving sentences, paragraphs, or pages around with ease, and trying several versions. Nothing is printed until you are satisfied that it is ready to print. The various versions of a paper can be saved easily. You no longer hesitate to make major changes during the editing process, since major changes no longer involve extensive retyping. You really have to use the equipment to appreciate how much time it saves and how easy it is to draft and edit a text on the screen.

All these advantages are true of word-processing equipment in general. In addition, there are several specialized programs that can provide assistance to the writer. For example, there are outlining programs that facilitate the organization of ideas, programs that can check your spelling or arrange footnotes at the bottom of the page, and graphics programs that facilitate the design of diagrams and graphs. New programs are developed every day; by the time you read this section, new programs will have been developed that will enable the writer to perform other time-consuming tasks easily. The basic advantages of the equipment, however, are the ability to draft quickly and edit your copy as extensively and as many times as you want without constant retyping, and the assurance that your final copy will be printed exactly the way you set it up on the screen, without any new misspellings or typographical errors.

THE WRITER'S RESPONSIBILITY

Having noted the wondrous efficiency of word-processing programs, I must also point out that computers are not magical machines capable of producing papers with no effort on the part of the writer. The ability to edit with ease means that there is even less excuse for a sloppy paper produced on word-processing equipment than there is for a paper that has been handwritten and then typed.

In fact, unless one knows how to use word-processing equipment correctly, there is no advantage to it at all. If students still write out their drafts in longhand and then use word-processing equipment to type the final copy, without doing any editing, they are not taking advantage of the technology, and the equipment has been reduced to an expensive typewriter. *There is no point in using word-processing equipment unless you take advantage of the capability for unlimited editing.* Remember that computers are literal and impartial. If your draft is a mess, the computer will not edit it for you but will dutifully print out your version, complete with all your grammatical errors, misspellings, and awkward constructions.

The most efficient way to use the equipment is to compose your draft on the keyboard, edit it on the screen, and then print out the revised final version. To use the power of a word-processing program to its full advantage, then, you need two separate skills. First, you need the ability to compose at the keyboard. Some people find this difficult, since they have been trained to use a typewriter only for copying text, not for composing. It is easier to make the transition from composing at a typewriter to composing on a computer keyboard than it is to change from writing your draft in longhand to composing at a keyboard. The second ability you need is knowledge of the specific program you are using and facility in putting it to work for you. You cannot edit without some facility in moving around the screen and using the various commands that delete characters, words, and lines. You need to know how to correct misspellings and typographical errors, how to add material in the middle of existing text, how to move sentences and sections around, and in general how to put all the abilities built into the program to work for you. Some programs are more complicated than others; it takes time and effort to learn a word-processing program. Most users can tell horror stories of mistakes they made, text they lost, and problems they ran into in the early stages of using a new program. Once you have invested the time necessary to learn a program, you then save time as you write with it; the more you write, the more time you save. If you spend all your time looking up commands or trying to figure out how to get out of the technical corners in which you find yourself, or if you live in perpetual terror of error messages flashing on the screen or of the computer's destroying your precious manuscript, then you are not saving any time. There is no point in using sophisticated equipment until you know how to make it do what you want it to do, rather than being at the mercy of the machine.

One result of the widespread use of word-processing equipment is that instructors now hear new excuses for late papers. Instead of "The baby spit up on my paper," or "The dog ate my draft," now we hear "We had a power surge or something—the screen went blank, and I lost my whole paper," or "My roommate had a party, and some idiot spilled clam dip on my disk." These new tales of woe are no more convincing than the old ones, because it is easy to learn how to avoid these dangers.

FORMAT ISSUES

The writer cannot assume that the built-in or "default" format automatically set up by a word-processing program is an acceptable format for college papers. Many programs, for example, use more space for text on a page than one should in a formal paper. Chapter 6 will discuss proper format in more detail; one is supposed to leave a margin of an inch and a half at the left, and at least an inch at the right, the top, and the bottom. That space is for your professor, who needs room to write comments, and also for standardization. Therefore, you have to know how to change the page layout and how to set up the margins you want.

Not all programs automatically number the pages in the proper way. The title page of a paper should not be numbered; preliminary pages should be numbered with lowercase roman numerals. Within the body of the paper, arabic page numbers should be placed at the top right-hand edge of the block of text, or in the center, at the top margin. You need to know the proper commands to instruct the printer to do this for you. You also might want to take advantage of the ability to print a heading automatically on each page. Tables, columns, and indented material may be complicated to arrange but will come out looking quite professional. In any program, there is usually a way to achieve the effects you want, but it may take some time to get things to come out right. Remember that the *writer* is supposed to be in control, not the computer.

EDITING

The chief advantage of word processing is the ability to edit extensively and repeatedly without retyping. Although most of your editing can be done on the screen, for some kinds of editing you may want to print a draft so that you can edit on paper ("hard copy," in the usual jargon) rather than on the screen. When you want to compare widely separated sections, for example, it may be easier to lay the pages side by side than to scroll through a long file on the screen or move around among several files. The best way to do the final editing may be with the aid of a preliminary printed copy. Otherwise, you may find when the text is printed that the "final" version still needs some work.

PRINTING

Computer-driven printers vary enormously in speed and quality, from dot-matrix printers and "letter-quality" daisy-wheel printers to the laser printers that rival printed books in clarity and appearance. If you have any doubt about whether the copy produced by a particular printer will be acceptable to your instructor, check with him or her, bringing a sample of the printer's work. Even if a particular printer does acceptable work, be sure you have a good ribbon. Some students use their ribbons far too long, so that the copies produced by their printers are much too faint.

Although most printers produce copy that would be acceptable to most instructors, there is some equipment that is not suitable for college papers.

Avoid the dot-matrix printers that cannot print the downward strokes of lowercase letters like *g* and *p* below the line; reading papers in which every *p* or *g* in the middle of a word looks like a capital is difficult and annoying. Some dot-matrix printers produce copy that is too fuzzy and blurred to read easily and cannot be clearly photocopied. Some printers justify the right-hand margin by inserting long and unequal spaces between words, rather than varying the spaces between letters. Reading several pages printed in this way can be tiring and annoying to the eye. If your printer works that way, you should shut off right-hand justification when printing a paper, opting for a "ragged" right margin rather than unevenly spaced words and odd-looking pages.

These issues may not be relevant for long, granting the rapid pace at which word-processing programs are developed and improved. In any case, find out as soon as possible if the equipment you plan to use will produce a paper that is acceptable in appearance and format to your instructor.

Finally, provided that you keep the disk on which your paper is stored, it may not be necessary to photocopy your paper in order to keep a "hard copy" in your files. You can always print another copy should you need one for any reason—in fact, you can even revise your paper further before sending an improved version to a graduate school as a sample of your work. Manufacturers of disks maintain that files stored on disks are perfectly safe, provided that you follow the instructions about storing your disks safely. On the other hand, disks can get lost, and files have been known to disappear from disks. You may feel more secure making a second hard copy for your files or submitting a photocopy and keeping the original printout for your files.

CONCLUSION

Word-processing equipment is a powerful tool that greatly facilitates the process of writing, editing, and printing a paper. It does not, however, eliminate the hard work of writing or the responsibility to edit and polish your work. However one produces a rough draft, it is still true that no one writes perfect drafts. What we said at the conclusion of the last chapter is true of papers produced with the aid of word-processing equipment, just as it is of papers produced the old way. The quality and effectiveness of your paper will be in direct proportion to the time and effort you put into careful editing.

chapter 6

Questions of Format

Whether a paper is typed or is produced on a word processor, there are standard rules about the way it should look. You may not see the point of these rules or agree with all of them, but there are practical reasons for most of them. Whether or not they make sense does not really matter; you must follow standard practice if you are interested in demonstrating professional competence. Remember the analogy between recital etiquette and standards for scholarly papers. In both cases, if you want your hard work to be taken seriously, you must follow accepted practice.

In general, the format for a research paper is the same in most fields, although some areas of study have developed their own ways of dealing with format issues. In the social sciences, for example, it is customary to place notes within the text, referring to numbered works listed in the bibliography. In this chapter we will discuss the standard format for papers in the arts and humanities, as well as the special problems of referring to music. Note that there are usually several ways to handle certain details, all within the range of correct standards.

There are three basic principles to remember about format questions. First, *be consistent*. If you follow Turabian's model for one footnote, then follow it for all your footnotes. Second, *be logical*; the purpose of footnotes and bibliographies is to be helpful to the reader. Be sure that your notes are helpful rather than confusing, and if you cannot find a model for a particular situation in one of the standard style manuals, pick the most logical and helpful way to handle the question. Third, *check with your instructor*; if your instructor insists that you follow one particular style manual, you need to know that early in the process of writing your paper. If the choice of a guide is up to you, follow the *Chicago Manual of Style;* it is clearly the most authoritative guide. The important thing to most instructors is that you follow an acceptable format and that you are consistent and logical in the way you deal with details. The worst offenses are inconsistency and carelessness.

PAPER

College papers should be typed on one side only on plain white paper of standard size, eight-and-a-half by eleven inches. You need not follow the special rules about paper for theses and dissertations; there is no particular reason to use paper of a particular weight or special thesis paper with blue lines marking the borders of the text. Lined sheets ripped from a notebook, with the shredded perforations still attached, are not acceptable. Save your colored paper for correspondence; lavender or buff paper is out of place for a research project and is regarded as an affectation, like brown or green ink.

Any plain white typing paper is acceptable, with a few exceptions. Lightweight "onion skin" paper may be difficult to read, especially if it is somewhat transparent. Avoid so-called erasable bond, which is difficult to write comments on and annoying to read, since the typed letters rub off on the reader's hand or sleeve. Your deathless prose can disappear too easily into oblivion. Any decent plain white typing paper will do; paper manufactured for copy machines is fine, too, and sturdier than most typing paper.

PAGE FORMAT

Formal papers are supposed to have standard margins. The left-hand margin is supposed to be one-and-a-half inches wide. The other three sides (right, top, and bottom) are supposed to have margins of at least one inch; some guides specify an inch and a half for them too. That means that *nothing* can extend into these margins; if the footnotes are placed at the bottom of the page, a standard margin must be left blank below the last footnote on the page.

There are two practical reasons for these standard margins. First, the reader needs some space in which to write editorial comments. Second, the standard margins provide an easy gauge of the length of a paper. A double-spaced typed page with standard margins contains about 250 words; it is useful for writers, professors, and publishers to know that a 5,000-word paper, for example, will be twenty pages long. If you have to read a paper to a group, you can assume that it will take about two minutes to read a standard page, and gauge the proper length of your paper accordingly.

SPACING

The text of your paper should be *double-spaced*. Many typewriters and printers have several options for spacing, and a page of text with one-and-a-half spaces between lines looks quite attractive. The standard practice, however, is still to double-space the text.

In papers, footnotes and bibliography entries are usually *single-spaced*. The practice is different when one submits an article for publication; publishers often want the notes and the bibliographies double-spaced like the text. Follow the recommendation of the style guide you use.

PAGE NUMBERS

The pages of your paper must be numbered in the following way. The title page is not numbered, nor is the optional extra blank sheet you might insert between title page and text. In the case of long papers, introductory material (preface, dedication, table of contents) is numbered with lowercase roman numerals—i, ii, iii, and so forth. The reason for this different numbering system is that those sections are often written last, after the main body of text is completed. In most undergraduate papers, the text begins immediately after the title page, without preliminary sections; the first page of text is page 1. Within the text, arabic numerals are used, and they are placed at the top margin, either in the upper right-hand corner, one double-space above the top line of text, or at the center of the page. The pages are numbered consecutively through the whole paper, including appendixes, notes, and bibliography. If the paper is divided into chapters, the numbering does not begin again with each chapter but continues consecutively through the entire paper. If you use a word processor to produce your paper, find out how to arrange the numbering in this fashion, or number the pages by hand.

When your paper is complete, you may want to staple the pages together, or insert the paper into one of the covers or folders sold for this purpose, so that the pages stay together and in the proper order. Remember that the instructor will probably read a large number of papers at one time; loose pages or slippery paper clips can create confusion and mix up your pages with someone else's project.

QUOTATIONS

The proper format for quotations seems to cause problems for many students. First of all, direct quotations must be clearly marked. Citing the exact words of another author without quotation marks or a footnote acknowledging your source is unethical; see the discussion of plagiarism in Chapter 3. Different kinds of quotations are handled in different ways.

Brief Quotations

Quotations that are short—defined in the various guides as less than three full lines, or five, or ten—are integrated into the body of the text and placed in quotation marks. For example:

Rosen finds the term "recapitulation" misleading. "If we use it to mean a simple repeat of the exposition with the secondary material put into the tonic, then the whole idea must be thrown out as unclassical: this type of recapitulation is the exception rather than the rule in the mature works of Haydn, Mozart, and Beethoven."[1]

1. Charles Rosen, The Classical Style (New York: W. W. Norton & Co., 1972), p. 75.

For now, ignore the footnote; our concern here is the format for the quotation itself. Note that the material cited must be quoted *exactly*, with the author's spelling and punctuation intact. One might argue that Rosen should have used a semicolon rather than a colon after "unclassical," but when quoting another author, the writer must quote exactly. Note the order of the punctuation marks after the quotation: period, quotation marks, superscript footnote number, space.

Ellipsis and Editorial Additions

If you omit some words from a direct quotation, accuracy demands that you signal that omission by the use of three spaced periods to show where material was left out.

As Rosen points out, "If we use it to mean a simple repeat of the exposition . . . then the whole idea must be thrown out as unclassical."[1]

Be very careful in your use of ellipsis. The preceding example is *wrong*, since Rosen obviously does not mean to say that the recapitulation is a simple repeat of the exposition. The omitted qualifying phrase, "with the secondary material put into the tonic," is essential to the sense of the quotation. Even when ellipsis does not misrepresent what the original author wrote, it can be confusing and can weaken the force of your argument. The alert reader naturally wonders exactly what was left out, why it was left out, and how the omitted material might change the force of the quotation.

If you want to add something to a quotation for the sake of clarity, you must make clear to the reader that you are doing so, by putting the editorial comment in *brackets*—not parentheses. Such insertions may be necessary to supply contextual material that is not clear in the isolated sentence cited. Brackets are the universal signal of editorial additions. Without them, you are misquoting the cited author, creating the impression that the insertion is part of the direct quotation. If you do not have brackets on your typewriter or printer, draw them in by hand. If you wish to clarify what Rosen means by "it" in the above quotation, for example, you must enclose your added antecedent in brackets.

> *Wrong:* If we use it—the term recapitulation—to mean a simple repeat of the exposition . . .
> *Wrong:* If we use it (recapitulation) to mean a simple repeat of the exposition . . .
> *Correct:* If we use it [recapitulation] to mean a simple repeat of the exposition . . .

Sic

There is a special editorial comment one can insert within quotations to let the reader know that the writer is quoting the source exactly and that whatever "mistakes" appear in the text are the responsibility of the cited author, not the writer. The Latin word *sic* ("thus") is inserted in brackets after an apparent error, to mean "It appears thus in the source." Since *sic* is a complete Latin word, not an abbreviation, it is not followed by a period. Thus:

> Thomas Morley, in *A Plaine and Easie Introduction to Practicall Musicke* [*sic*], takes a somewhat different approach.

In this case, the use of *sic* seems unnecessary and pretentious. Anyone who knows about Elizabethan English is aware that spelling at that time was delightfully erratic. The *sic* therefore seems overly cautious. There are situations, however, in which this device is useful. When you are sure, for example, that a date in a quotation is wrong, you might want to use *sic* so that the reader understands that you are aware of the error. Some experts would set *sic* in standard type, rather than in italics (underlining in typescript); the *Chicago Manual of Style* (6.59) recommends italics.

Long Quotations

Long quotations—anything more than three lines, or five, or ten, depending on which guide you follow—must be set off from the body of your text. Long quotations are started on a new line, single-spaced (according to most style guides), and indented. Style guides vary in describing how far to indent long quotations; some say five spaces, some say as many as ten. If the opening of the quotation is the beginning of a paragraph, the first line should be indented further, like the opening line of any paragraph. When long quotations are arranged on the page in this way, there is no mistaking that the quoted material is separate from your own text. For that reason, quotation marks are not needed in long quotations; the appearance of the page makes clear that they are not the writer's own words. Since there are no quotation marks around the whole citation, material in quotation marks within the cited material is put in *double* quotation marks. Although it is possible to introduce a long quotation with an incomplete sentence, such as "As Rosen says," and then start the long quotation on a new line, that method seems awkward. It is better to introduce the quotation with a complete sentence.

Whenever you are contemplating including a long quotation in your paper, stop and think about its effectiveness. It is generally possible to achieve the same effect in other ways, such as paraphrasing or summarizing the content of most of the quotation, and then citing one particularly strong sentence or phrase from the source. On the other hand, the long quotation may be the best way to make your point. In that case, as in so many others, moderation is the rule. If you use too many long quotations, then you create the impression that you are stringing quotations together rather than communicating the results of your own research and thought.

Whether quotations are short or long, the most important goal is *clarity*. The reader must know which words are quoted and which are yours; you must quote your sources precisely, with footnotes telling the reader exactly where he or she may find that citation; and you must make sure that the reader knows where editorial additions or deletions have been made. Judicious quotations can be very effective in a research paper, but the writer must know how to handle all the details of format so that the quotations are gracefully integrated into the text of the paper.

FOOTNOTE FORMAT

Footnotes are numbered consecutively throughout a paper, and each note is numbered to correspond with the superscript number that appears in the text. Whether notes are typed (or printed) at the bottom of the page or grouped together following the text, their form is the same. The first reference to a publication must be complete; later references can be shortened, provided that enough information is included to make clear to the reader where the citation can be found. We will discuss the first reference to various types of publications, and then subsequent shorter references.

First Reference

Books The first footnote referring to a book must include the following information: author's name, first name first; the title of the book, underlined; the name of the editor or the translator, if any; the edition, if there is more than one, and number of volumes, if there is more than one; place of publication, name of publisher, and date of publication, all in parentheses; and page or pages on which the cited information appears. Study the following footnote, which appeared earlier in our discussion of quotations.

1. Charles Rosen, The Classical Style (New York: W. W. Norton & Co., 1971), p. 75.

Every detail of this format is important, including the punctuation and the spaces. If there are multiple authors, all are listed first, in the same order as they appear on the title page. The full title must be listed exactly as it appears in the book, complete with subtitle and correct capitalization. Book titles are always underlined in typed papers; underlining is the equivalent in typescript of printed italics. Correct capitalization of foreign titles can be somewhat complicated. All nouns are capitalized in German; thus, German titles are cited with the nouns capitalized and other words in lowercase letters. In French titles, capitalize only the first word and all proper names. Follow the same practice in Latin and Italian titles. When foreign proper names or titles appear in a footnote, you must include all accent marks, umlauts, and diacritical marks. *Without all these marks, the name or the title is misspelled.* You may have to draw in these marks by hand after the paper is typed; in that case, use a pen with a fine point and ink as close as possible in color to the typed letters. Even if the marks are obviously added by hand, they are still required.

Subtitles are another interesting question. In Rosen's book, for example, a subtitle, set in different type from the main title, appears on the title page, with no punctuation between the main title and the subtitle. When you cite the full title, add a colon between title and subtitle, thus:

The Classical Style: Haydn, Mozart, Beethoven

The publication information can also raise some questions. The rule about place of publication is that well-known cities are identified by the name of the city alone, whereas less well known cities need to be further identified by including an abbreviation for the state. See *Chicago Manual*, 16.70. Thus, New York, Paris, and London can stand by themselves (unless you mean Paris, Texas), but the correct way to list the place of publication for works published by Prentice-Hall is Englewood Cliffs, N.J., rather than just Englewood Cliffs.

University presses raise an interesting question. The Indiana University Press, for example, is in Bloomington, where the university is. It hardly seems necessary to list the state twice, since it also appears in the name of the publishing house. I find the following listing sufficient:

Bloomington: Indiana University Press, 1962.

Technically, since Bloomington is not a major city like New York or London, the citation should read as follows:

Bloomington, Ind.: Indiana University Press.

In this special case, common sense and the principle of avoiding redundancy seem to override the general rule.

It is sufficient to list one city, even if several appear on the title page. Look at the publishing information in the front of any volume of the *New Grove Dictionary*. Macmillan, the publisher, is a huge conglomerate, with offices in London, New York, Sydney, and several other cities. Do not list all those cities in your footnote; "London" is enough.

There are two approaches to correct listing of the publisher's name in a footnote or bibliography. One is to shorten the name as much as possible, provided that the publisher is clearly identified. In this system, instead of "W. W. Norton & Co., Inc.," one can simply write "Norton," on the grounds that the company is well known. This approach is consistent with the trend toward simplifying citations, and makes it easier to be consistent when citing foreign publishers.

The other approach insists on citing the publisher's name exactly as it appears on the title page. In that case, one must include the full title and carefully follow details of spelling and punctuation. The following examples illustrate this sort of citation.

W. W. Norton & Co., Inc. (with an ampersand, not "and")

Simon & Schuster (with an ampersand, not "and")

Harcourt Brace Jovanovich (no commas, no "and")

The *Chicago Manual of Style* recommends citing a publisher's name as it appears on the title page, omitting the initial "The" and "Inc." or its foreign equivalents at the end (16.76) and allows use of either an ampersand (&) or "and" (16.79). I recommend that you follow the *Chicago Manual* unless your instructor insists on a different guide; whatever system you follow, follow it consistently.

As a general rule, when listing the date of a publication, list the date of the latest revision or of the edition you used. If no date of publication is given, even in the copyright information, you may use the abbreviation *n.d.* ("no date") in place of the date in the footnote, or simply close the parentheses after the publisher's name. Listing the date of some types of publications, such as translations and reprints of older books, can get complicated. The *Chicago Manual of Style* (16.57) points out that the writer should use his or her own judgment in some situations. It makes little sense to list only the dates of modern editions of works like Charles Burney's eyewitness accounts of the musical situation in the eighteenth century; in that case, I would list both the date of the original publication and the date of the modern edition I consulted. One other example will illustrate how complex these questions can become. In 1962, Raymond Haggh published a translation of Books I and II of Hugo Riemann's *History of Music Theory,* first published in German in 1898, adding a preface, commentary, and notes that update much of the information. In 1974 the Da Capo Press published a reprint of the Haggh translation. In this case, I think it is sufficient to cite the translation and reprint without listing the title and date of the original publication. This footnote could take many forms; I would list the work as follows.

Hugo Riemann, History of Music Theory, trans., with a preface, commentary, and notes, by Raymond Haggh (Lincoln, Neb.: University of Nebraska Press, 1962; reprint, Da Capo Press, 1974).

A footnote should also include a listing of the specific page or pages to which you are referring, unless you want to refer to the whole book, as in the case of a general reference to a biography. For a single page, type "p," period, space, and the page number. For several pages, "pp. 24–29" or "pp. 24–9" is clearer than the alternative "pp. 24ff." signifying "page 24 and the following pages." All footnotes end with a period.

Articles Articles, whether they appear in collections, journals, or reference works, are dealt with in a different manner from the format for books. Titles of articles are put in quotation marks, and the title of the collection or journal is underlined. The title of the collection or reference work is followed by its publication information (place: publisher, date). The particular issue of a journal is identified by volume, year, and the pages on which the article may be found. Note the format of the following examples.

1. Charles Van den Borren, "Dufay and His School," in Ars Nova and the Renaissance, ed. Dom Anselm Hughes and Gerald Abraham, Vol. III of New Oxford History of Music (London: Oxford University Press, 1960), 214–238.

This example is interesting because the collection in which the article appears is itself one volume of a larger series. There are several other ways to list this information. The order used here makes clear that Hughes and Abraham are the editors of Volume III, not of the whole series. What is not clear in this format is that 1960 is the date of publication for Volume III, not for the whole series, volumes of which appeared in different years. One must rely on the rules about logic and consistency.

Articles in journals are easier to deal with. Study the following typical footnote entry.

> 1. Ellen Rosand, "Seneca and the Interpretation of L'Incoronazione di Poppea," Journal of the American Musicological Society 38 (1985), 34–71.

Several details of this entry deserve comment. First, note that within the title of the article, the title of the opera is underlined, since it is the title of a major work. The title of the article is in quotation marks, and the journal's name is underlined.

Individual issues of periodicals can be identified in several ways. At the bottom of the title page of that issue of the journal, the following information appears.

Volume XXXVIII   Spring 1985   Number 1

We do not need all that information. Journals are usually paginated consecutively through an entire year, and back issues are bound, a year's issues in each volume, before they are stored on the library shelves. Therefore, the number of the issue and other identifying information, like the season of the year, are not necessary. Besides, journals use several different systems to identify the separate issues within a year. All the reader needs is the volume number, year, and page number, because that information is sufficient to locate the article. Arabic numerals are preferable to roman numerals for the volume numbers, since some journals have been in business for a long time and roman numerals get cumbersome over twenty or so. The words *volume* and *page* are not necessary; the first number is obviously the volume, since it is followed by the year. Therefore, the other number is the page. Alternative ways to list the volume, year, and page numbers are given below; see the *Chicago Manual* 16.98–123 for further details.

> 1. . . . Journal of the American Musicological Society 38: 34–71 (1986). Or . . . XXXVIII, pp. 34–71 (1986).

Whichever system you follow, there is no need for any other information, such as Fall, Number 3, or the words *volume* and *page*.

Dictionaries and encyclopedias Citing articles in dictionaries and encyclopedias is somewhat more confusing. The *Chicago Manual of Style* (17.62) recommends listing the *title* of the reference work first; then the edition number; then the specific article, introduced by the abbreviation *s.v.*, meaning *sub verbo*, Latin for "under the word." Thus, a reference to the article "Mode" in the *New Grove* would read as follows:

> 1. Stanley Sadie, ed., <u>New Grove Dictionary of Music and Musicians</u> (London: Macmillan, 1980); s.v. "Mode," Vol. XII, pp. 376–450.

That format is certainly correct as it stands; some guides recommend leaving out the publication information in parentheses, since the work is a standard reference. *Vol.* could be left out, especially if you use a roman numeral for the volume number; the last phrase could read as follows:

> . . . s.v. "Mode," XII, 376–450.
>
> *Or:* . . . s.v. "Mode," Vol. 12, pp. 376–450.

That system, while correct, works best for referring to short unsigned articles. It is less appropriate for reference to the *New Grove*, however, because the articles in the *New Grove* are extended pieces, the size of journal articles or monographs—note the length of the "Mode" article, equivalent in size to a small book. Second, the author of the article is not named in that format, and the *New Grove* articles were written by acknowledged experts, and signed; the author's name appears at the end of the article. There is another system for signed articles in reference works, which treats them more like articles in journals, with the name of the author of the article listed first. In this system, the *New Grove* article on mode would be listed as follows:

> 1. Harold Powers, "Mode," in Stanley Sadie, ed., <u>New Grove Dictionary of Music and Musicians</u> (London: Macmillan, 1980), XII, 376–450.

The advantage of this second format is its emphasis on the author. One usually finds that the authors of *New Grove* articles have written other books or articles on the same subject; the same authors' names will appear in several places in the footnotes. When one gets to the bibliography, where items are alphabetized by authors' last names, the reader sees all the published work by a single author listed in one place, *New Grove* articles along with other publications.

The first system, listing the reference work first, then referring to a specific article, works well for shorter reference works, like *Baker's Biographical Dictionary*, in which all the articles are written by the same person. To refer the reader to the Baker's article on Bizet, for example, the note would read as follows:

> 1. Nicolas Slonimsky, ed., <u>Baker's Biographical Dictionary of Music and Musicians,</u> Seventh edition (New York: Schirmer, 1984); s.v. "Bizet, Georges," pp. 265–266.

Scores and recordings   It may be necessary, depending on the nature of your paper, to refer to specific scores and recordings, and there is a standard format for such references. For scores, list the composer's name first, then the title of the work, the editor or the edition, the publication information in parentheses, and the specific score page or measure numbers to which you wish to refer. Measure numbers are listed as follows: *m.* for "measure," *mm.* for "measures," then a space, then the number or numbers. You cannot use *ms.* to mean "measures," since *ms.* is the standard abbreviation for "manuscript." If the score has rehearsal numbers or letters, they, too, can be used as points of reference. If you can assume that the reader has at hand a standard edition of the work under discussion, you can specify a passage by listing page number, system, and measure, but measure numbers running consecutively through a movement are much clearer. The following note refers to the opening of Mahler's Fourth Symphony, as found in the miniature orchestral score published by Boosey & Hawkes.

> 1. Gustav Mahler, Symphony No. 4, Revised edition (London: Boosey & Hawkes, 1943), mm. 1–24. *Or:* pp. 3–5.

Titles of musical works   Straightforward titles of musical works, like Symphony No. 4 or *Night on Bald Mountain,* cause no particular problem for the writer. Some titles are more confusing, and a few hints about accepted practice may be helpful. Individual pieces or sections of a larger work are cited in quotation marks; the title of the larger work is underlined. Thus:

"Caro nome" from Verdi's <u>Rigoletto</u>
"The Great Gate of Kiev" from <u>Pictures at an Exhibition</u>
Schumann, "Mondnacht" from <u>Liederkreis</u>, Opus 39

Generic titles are capitalized when they are titles of specific works, and left in lowercase when used as generic nouns.

Haydn's Symphony No. 104 . . .
Haydn is best known for his symphonies and string quartets.

Subtitles added to generic titles are placed in quotation marks inside parentheses after the formal title of the work.

Haydn, Symphony No. 103 in E-flat Major ("Drum Roll")
Schubert, Quintet in A Major for Piano and Strings ("The Trout")

Those who market classical recordings sometimes add new nicknames to classical works in an attempt to capitalize on the popularity of films that have used those works as background music. Such nicknames, like Mozart's "Elvira Madigan" Piano Concerto or the "2001" Tone Poem of Strauss, obviously have no place in a serious paper.

Finally, when one must choose between several alternative versions of a title—Piano Concerto No. 24 in A Major, K. 488, or Concerto for Pianoforte and Orchestra in A Major, No. 24, K.V. 488, for example—the wisest practice is to cite the work exactly as it is listed in a reliable reference work, such as the *New Grove*, and to follow the general principles of clarity and consistency.

Sometimes one wishes to refer to a specific recording, especially if the paper compares different recordings or discusses the details of a particular recorded performance. To cite a recording, list the composer first, then the title of the work. Information about artists is optional, but one *must* list the record company and the company's reference number for that recording. A note referring to the Nonesuch recording of Mahler's Fourth Symphony would read like this:

> 1. Gustav Mahler, Symphony No. 4; Orchestra of the Berlin Radio, Lorin Maazel, Conductor; Heather Harper, Soprano (Nonesuch H-71259).

Or, more briefly:

> 1. Gustav Mahler, Symphony No. 4 (Nonesuch H-71259).

If you want to refer to signed liner notes accompanying a recording, they are listed as follows:

> 1. Jack Dieter, liner notes for Mahler, Symphony No. 4 (Nonesuch H-71259).

Reference to a booklet included with an album:

> 1. George Perle, notes for Schoenberg's Pierrot Lunaire, brochure for The Music of Arnold Schoenberg, Vol. I (Columbia M2S 679).

Citing scores and recordings can get complicated; in special situations, the principles of consistency, logic, and clarity will generally point the way to the correct format.

Shorter References

The complete form for footnotes must be used the first time a publication is referred to. Subsequent footnotes referring to the same publication can be much briefer; only the information necessary to direct the reader to the appropriate publication is included. Necessary information includes the author's *last* name, a short version of the title, and the page number. If several works by the same author have been cited, the short version of the title must clearly specify which of the works already cited is being referred to. Once the full information has been given in the first citation, the works listed previously can be referred to later as follows:

> 5. Rosen, <u>Classical Style</u>, 213–220.
> 6. Rosand, "Interpretation of <u>Poppea</u>," 64.
> 7. Van den Borren, "Dufay," <u>New Oxford History</u> III, 234–235.
> 8. Powers, "Mode," <u>New Grove</u> XII, 380.

Common sense and brevity are the rule in shorter references. Include enough information to identify the specific work and remind the reader that the work has already been cited, without being so cryptic that the reader does not know which work is being cited.

Op. cit., Art. cit., Loc. cit., Ibid.

Present usage seems to favor the short title in references after the first full footnote rather than the abbreviations that were customary some years ago (*Chicago Manual* 17.12). That is a welcome change, since the old abbreviations caused considerable confusion for both writers and readers. In case one still chooses to use them, a word of explanation about each one is in order.

Op. cit. is an abbreviation for the Latin words *opere citato*, meaning "in the work cited." Since both words are abbreviated, each is followed by a period, and neither word is capitalized, unless the phrase begins the footnote, in which case the *O* is capitalized.

> 5. Rosen, op. cit., p. 47.

This abbreviation can be used *only* when a book by Rosen has been cited in a previous footnote, where the full title and publication information have been listed. It cannot be used when more than one work by the same author has been cited previously.

Art. cit. is an analogous abbreviation, meaning "in the article cited," assuming that only one article by that author has been cited previously. Thus:

> 6. Rosand, art. cit., p. 64.

Loc. cit. stands for the Latin *loco citato*, "in the place cited." It is difficult to use this abbreviation correctly, since it is not always clear whether the "place" referred to is the previously cited book or article or the specific pages already referred to.

Ibid. is an abbreviation for the Latin *ibidem*, meaning "in the same place." Standard style guides list restrictions on the use of this abbreviation (*Chicago Manual* 17.13); some would permit its use only when it refers to the immediately preceding note and the two references appear on the same page, so that the reader can easily check to see which work is referred to. *Ibid.* was the most useful of these abbreviations and still is used more than the others.

The present preference for short titles in the second reference rather than these abbreviations is perfectly logical. "Rosen, Classical Style" immediately conveys more information than "Rosen, op. cit." It directs the reader to a well-known work, without forcing him or her to work through the intermediate step of recalling which of Rosen's works was cited earlier. *Op. cit., art. cit., loc. cit.,* and *ibid.* are now considered old-fashioned, or at least are used rarely. In this case, change is welcome; the new practice is much simpler and clearer.

Abbreviations for Frequently Cited Works

It may be useful in long papers, such as theses and dissertations, to include a table of abbreviations in the introductory material or at the beginning of the bibliography, so that the writer is freed from the obligation of writing out long titles each time a work is cited. Research papers at the undergraduate level are not likely to be long enough to need tables of abbreviations, but the practice of using abbreviations for works cited frequently can sometimes be useful. Before the publication of the *New Grove Dictionary*, for example, *Die Musik in Geschichte und Gegenwart* was the standard reference work in music history; it was widely known as MGG, so that a writer could use that as an abbreviation *after* listing the formal title and the publication information in the first citation. The problem with abbreviations is that, like other jargon, they are standard only within a small community. Among scholars who work with medieval music theory, for example, CSM stands for *Corpus Scriptorum de Musica*, a collection of critical editions of theory treatises. That abbreviation is not standard, however, even among musicologists; therefore, one would still need to list the full title in the first reference, perhaps with a note that the title will hereafter be abbreviated.

A few words of caution are in order about using abbreviations. First, no abbreviation can be used in a footnote (or anywhere else) until it has first been explained. Second, there is no reason to invent an abbreviation unless the title will come up frequently; if there are only one or two references to the work, it is not worth the trouble to create and explain an abbreviation. Last, one should avoid fanciful or idiosyncratic abbreviations that may confuse the reader. Initials of titles, like MGG, JAMS, and MQ, are often used as standard abbreviations (for *Die Musik in Geschichte und Gegenwart, Journal of the American Musicological Society,* and *Musical Quarterly*) because they are clear. A first-reference footnote establishing an abbreviation for later use might read like the following.

> 1. In this paper we will be comparing the editions of the Concerto found in the Bach-Gesellschaft Edition (hereafter BGA) (city: publisher, date) and the Neue Bach-Ausgabe (hereafter NBA) (city: publisher, date).

In summary, do not bother to establish abbreviations unless the works are cited frequently. Above all, abbreviations must be clear and should readily call to mind the titles for which they stand.

BIBLIOGRAPHY FORMAT

In the previous chapter we discussed what should be included in your bibliography and the relationship between the footnotes and the bibliography. Now we turn our attention to bibliography format.

The first question to address is the *order* of items. Bibliographies are arranged in alphabetical order by authors' last names, or by first words of titles when no author is listed. The writer may choose to divide the bibliography into different categories by dividing books and articles from scores and recordings, or primary materials from secondary sources, or perhaps books from articles. If one divides the bibliography into categories, then the proper order is alphabetical by author within each category.

The proper format for bibliography entries is different in several respects from that for footnotes. One immediate difference is indention. The first line of a footnote is indented, and subsequent lines are flush with the left margin. The reverse is true in bibliography entries; the first line is flush with the left margin, and subsequent lines are indented one tab stop, like a paragraph. In general, the same information is listed in the bibliography as in the first or full footnote, but the format is different.

Books

In a bibliography entry for a book, the following items are included, in this form: author's *last* name, comma, first name, period. In the case of multiple authors, the *Chicago Manual* (16.15) recommends listing the second author first name first.

> Jones, John, and Howard Smith.

Some other guides prefer using the same order for all authors.

Jones, John, and Smith, Howard.

Here, as elsewhere, follow one style guide consistently.
Next comes the title, underlined in typescript, followed by a period.
Then the publication information, *without* parentheses, in the same form as
in a footnote—that is, city, colon, publisher, comma, date, period.
Rosen's *Classical Style* would be listed thus in a bibliography:

Rosen, Charles. The Classical Style. New York: W. W. Norton & Co., 1971.

Articles

Similar changes are made in bibliography listings of articles, whether
they appear in collections, journals, or reference works. The articles listed in
the section on footnote format would be listed in this way in a bibliography:

Powers, Harold. "Mode." Stanley Sadie, ed., New Grove Dictionary of Music
and Musicians. London: Macmillan, 1980. Volume 12, pp. 376–450. *Or:* XII,
376–450.

Rosand, Ellen. "Seneca and the Interpretation of L'Incoronazione di Poppea."
Journal of the American Musicological Society 38 (1965), 34–71.

Van den Borren, Charles. "Dufay and His School." Ars Nova and the Renaissance, 1300–1540, ed. Dom Anselm Hughes and Gerald Abraham. Volume
III of The New Oxford History of Music. London: Oxford University Press,
1960.

Multiple Items by the Same Author

Following the general principle of omitting unnecessary information, one need not retype the author's name if a second entry by the same
author immediately follows an entry in which the name has been spelled
out. One simply types a line of several spaces (the *Chicago Manual* specifies
"an unbroken line three ems long," and other guides specify a line of as
few as five or seven or as many as fifteen units) followed by a period. The
Campbell guide recommends a continuous line made of seven units of
the *underline* character; the *Chicago Manual* shows an unbroken *dash*,
impossible to duplicate on most typewriters, since repeated strokes of the
hyphen character will not produce a continuous line. However you make
it, that line substitutes for the author's last and first names and is followed
by a period, if the title comes next, or by a comma and the co-author's
name. If there are several entries by the same author, they are arranged
in alphabetical order by title.
The following set of entries illustrates the proper format for multiple
entries by the same author.

Bukofzer, Manfred. "English Church Music of the Fifteenth Century." <u>Ars Nova and the Renaissance</u>, ed. Dom Anselm Hughes and Gerald Abraham. Volume III of <u>The New Oxford History of Music</u>. London: Oxford University Press, 1960.

————. <u>Music in the Baroque Era</u>. New York: W. W. Norton & Co., 1947.

————, and John Jones. "Popular Music of Fifteenth-Century England." <u>Musical Quarterly</u> 62 (1949), 23–46.

The same general principles apply to bibliography entries as apply to footnotes. First, be consistent; choose a specific format recommended by one of the standard guides and follow it consistently. Second, use common sense when dealing with special problems or questions that are not specifically treated in the standard guides. Include enough information to direct the reader to the sources you used; do not add useless or irrelevant information. Study the format for footnotes and bibliographies; once you are aware of the information you need to include, you will be more likely to write down the appropriate information about each source you encounter in your research. Once you get into the habit of following a standard format, you will find that it is much easier to follow that pattern consistently than it is to invent your own idiosyncratic and perhaps unacceptable system each time you write a paper.

CONCLUSION

This chapter has devoted considerable space to questions of format. Still, we have discussed only a few basic issues; look through the *Chicago Manual of Style* if you think this chapter is overly detailed. There are many issues we have not even touched upon; the number of potential questions regarding footnote and bibliography format is theoretically infinite.

The central point to bear in mind is that there is a proper way to type and present a paper. If you submit a paper scrawled on sheets torn from notebooks or typed on several different typewriters and covered with blobs of correction fluid or messy corrections, or if you invent your own format for footnotes and bibliography entries or skip the notes and the bibliography altogether, you cannot expect your paper to be taken seriously. There is an accepted format for research papers, and your work will not be taken seriously, or may not be read at all, until you learn to present it in acceptable fashion. At the moment, your profession is to be a college student. Knowledge of the proper format for your research papers is one of the tools of your present "trade," and one of the ways in which you demonstrate your professional competence and ability to meet the exacting standards of the world in which you have chosen to compete.

chapter 7

The Seminar Presentation

There are other kinds of assignments that involve some of the same challenges and skills as writing a convincing research paper. In addition, each of these tasks has its own special requirements; each, therefore, deserves some discussion. We will deal with seminar presentations, program notes, concert reviews, and essay examinations, each in a separate chapter.

Presenting a report in a seminar is in some ways the most difficult of academic assignments. Many of us feel intimidated by the thought of addressing any group, particularly a group of our peers. Some people have a knack for speaking in a natural, lively, and persuasive way; others tend to freeze in front of a group and hide behind an uninvolved, offhand manner that does little to engage the interest of their listeners.

Although it is not the place of this book to train persuasive public speakers, a few suggestions about how to approach an oral presentation may be helpful. It is important to realize that spoken style is different from written style and that the process of preparing for an oral presentation is different in some ways from the process of writing a convincing paper. We will discuss each step of the process.

RESEARCH

The process of locating material for a seminar presentation is exactly the same as the research process for a paper. The fact that an oral presentation has to work within strict time limits does not imply that one can shorten the research process. In fact, you might want to be especially thorough in doing research for a seminar presentation, since seminars usually involve a question-and-discussion period after each presentation. Even if your presentation is well researched and organized, you certainly want to avoid the embarrassment of being unable to answer the questions your classmates might raise and having to repeat lamely what you have already said. No research will go to waste, even if material you discover does not fit into the presentation. The research process was discussed in Chapter 3; start with the basic resources listed there—dictionaries and encyclopedias, histories, biographies, and thematic catalogs.

ORGANIZING THE PRESENTATION

Once you have completed your research, the process of turning a mass of information into a logical, coherent presentation is similar to the early stages of writing a paper. The first thing you need is a logical and fairly complete outline; review the section on outlining in Chapter 4. In the case of a seminar presentation, a coherent outline is even more critical than it is in a paper. In a paper, you can always add a few extra pages if you decide to discuss some additional material. In a seminar presentation, you usually have to stay within rigid time limits; the time you devote to an interesting digression is time taken away from your main point. As you plan and edit your outline, there are several issues peculiar to oral presentations that you should keep in mind.

Time Limits

Working within the time constraints is the key to planning an effective seminar presentation. Let us assume that the professor has allotted an hour to each presentation. You will probably have to stop after one hour, whether or not you have covered the material you planned to cover. Some students seem unable to stay within assigned time limits, and make unrealistic plans to cover much more than one can possibly cover in the allotted time. The first time you prepare an oral presentation, it may be difficult to estimate how much time each point will take and to decide if you can work through your entire outline in the allotted time. If you are not sure about the timing, have a dress rehearsal for a few students whose judgment you trust. Not only will you get a better sense of pace and timing; they can also tell you whether your presentation is clear and convincing and whether some sections need more work.

Recorded Examples

Assuming that your presentation deals with some aspect of musical style, you will want to illustrate your presentation with recorded musical examples. Because of the time limits, you need to be very selective about recorded musical examples; choose brief excerpts that clearly support what you are saying. A seminar presentation is not the appropriate time for a survey of a composer's greatest hits. I remember one presentation in which the student, unable to choose between excerpts, had prepared forty-five minutes of recorded excerpts to play during a one-hour presentation. Naturally, he was not able to finish his presentation. After dealing with about half of his planned outline, he trailed off lamely with a mumbled summary of what he would have covered if there had been enough time.

Recorded excerpts must be chosen very carefully and timed exactly. It makes sense to tape your excerpts rather than to fumble around with discs, trying to find the exact spot you want to play. Everything must be carefully planned if you want to take full advantage of the limited time you have. The time and effort you devote to preparing a tape will ensure that your presentation moves along briskly and creates a professional and convincing impression.

Writing Every Word versus Speaking from an Outline

As you edit and fine-tune your outline, you will need to decide whether you plan to speak from a detailed outline or write out every word and read your text. If the instructor insists on your reading a fully written-out text, then of course you are freed from making this decision. If not, consider the advantages and disadvantages of each system. Writing out the full text has the obvious advantage of ensuring that you will not have to fumble for the next word or idea. The disadvantage is that reading a paper is not the same thing as speaking to a group, and listening to someone read a paper can be deadly. I encourage students to work from a detailed outline. The obvious advantage is that your words seem more direct and spontaneous. Since no one but you will ever see either your outline or your text, it makes more sense to spend your preparation time refining your outline and preparing your recorded examples rather than drafting and editing a text. If you decide to speak from an outline, it should be a very detailed outline, so that you know exactly where you are going and how you plan to get there. You must know in advance exactly how you plan to begin and how you want to end. In fact, it may be advisable to write out your opening and closing words, so that you get under way smoothly, without fumbling around, and wrap up the presentation with a strong conclusion, rather than trailing off weakly with something like, "Well—that's about all I have to say." In your notes, you must also have all direct quotes written out, or whatever specific directions you need to find quotations or examples. It is deadly to sit through a long pause while the speaker fumbles around to find the passage he or she wants to read.

Preparing a Handout

As you work with your outline, deciding exactly what you want to cover and how you plan to proceed, you should consider assembling a handout of three or four pages to distribute to the class. There are several advantages to handouts. First, some kinds of information are extremely difficult to communicate orally. A selected bibliography, a list of the composer's works, and an outline of the main events of his life are much easier for your audience to read than to pick up by ear. If you wish, you are free to read a bibliography to a group, but you cannot realistically expect a listener to absorb that information. Besides, it is useful for the listeners to have a selective bibliography in their files, should they wish to return to the topic at some time in the future.

You might also consider including in your handout a selected musical example or two. If all members of the class have the same page of score in front of them, you can discuss specific details of musical style that you could not make clear by your words alone. As you put the handout together, you can mark the pages of music, drawing attention to the details that you plan to discuss.

Some students go to extremes in preparing their handouts for seminars, as if the grade for the presentation were determined by the size and cost of the handout. I have seen handouts of twenty or thirty pages, filled with fancy illustrations and page after page of photocopied score. It is extremely costly, and probably illegal, to make multiple copies of entire scores or movements. Be as selective with musical examples as you are with recorded examples; you can probably illustrate any stylistic point you wish to make by including a page or two of score or by creating your own diagrams or graphics to illustrate large-scale organization or structure. At the other extreme, some students provide a poorly typed page or two, perhaps including a hastily assembled bibliography in need of editing and proofreading. Anything you hand out with your name on it should be typed and edited with the same care that you would use on a research paper.

There are other ways besides handouts to provide scores for the class; one alternative is to bring multiple copies of the appropriate scores. If you choose this method, think about the logistics and keep the time constraints in mind. If the scores are different editions with different page numbers, or if some students will read a piano-vocal score and others an orchestral score, the members of the class may spend all their time trying to figure out where you are. If there are several short examples found in several different volumes, the whole presentation can turn into a complicated game of circulating and collecting scores, rather than listening to what you have to say. Once a stylistic point is made clear through detailed study of one musical example, it may be better to *listen* to other recorded examples rather than trying to provide a score for each recorded example. After all, music majors should be able to listen analytically and make stylistic judgments, particularly after their attention has been drawn to the stylistic point you are trying to illustrate. Difficult choices have to be made, just as they do in a paper; every example, whether it is a page from a score, a diagram, or a recorded example, must clearly support the point you are trying to make.

Once you have your outline, your plans for the handout, and your recorded examples clearly in mind, if you still have doubts about whether your plans are realistic, you may want to consult your instructor to see what he or she thinks of your plan. If you have been assigned the first presentation, you are at a disadvantage, because there is no prior model on which to pattern your presentation. In such a case, it is a particularly good idea for you to ask for the instructor's reaction to your plans for the presentation. The instructor should not be expected to do the work for you, but once you have done the work, he or she probably would be willing to tell you whether your plans seem realistic and whether you can accomplish what you wish to accomplish in the time allotted.

TONE AND APPROACH

Finally, as you prepare your outline and handout, and as the time for your presentation gets closer, think about the impression you want to create in your presentation. From your own experience sitting in class, you know the sort of approach that appeals to you. Remember that audiences generally approach a lecture or presentation with a willingness to listen. As long as the speaker seems to know what he or she is talking about, is well prepared, and is interested in communicating with you, you will listen. The audience's willingness to listen will last through the whole presentation, as long as the speaker does not interfere with that willingness by fumbling around, seeming bored or unprepared, or not knowing what is coming next. To hold the attention of a class, one need not be a superb public speaker. The only thing students cannot tolerate, as you well know, is to have their time wasted by anyone, faculty or student, who is not prepared or who does not seem to know or care what is coming next.

The feeling you want to communicate, then, is that you know what you are doing, you are interested in your topic, you have spent considerable time in research, and you will move crisply through your outline. You assume that the audience is interested in your topic, and you make clear that you will not waste their precious time. You are not standing in front of them as a preacher, exhorting them to some action, or as an entertainer, trying to amuse them for an hour. You are there as a competent professional, reporting on the insights and knowledge you have gained, sharing your vision of some specific musical works with them. If you have done the necessary research and planned your presentation carefully, and if you present yourself in this way, the experience will be a satisfying one for both you and your audience.

chapter 8

Program Notes

At some point during your life as a student, or later in the professional world, you will probably be asked to write program notes for a recital or a concert. Program notes present a special challenge to the writer because of their purpose and because of the severe space limitations under which one usually works.

THE PURPOSE OF PROGRAM NOTES

Program notes are different from research papers. Papers are written to prove the writer's competence as a scholar and, therefore, must include the standard scholarly apparatus of footnotes and bibliography. The purpose of program notes, on the other hand, is not directly scholarly, although whatever you write must be based on solid scholarly research and analysis. The purpose of program notes is to increase the listener's understanding of the music to be performed, and therefore his or her appreciation and enjoyment of the concert. If the listener has the opportunity in advance to learn something about the background of the piece, its special purpose, or the ways in which it is unique, he or she then has something specific to listen for and is less likely to sit passively, letting the music wash over him or her. Intelligent listeners appreciate informative and well-written program notes.

Writing for a Specific Audience

It is often difficult to gauge the background and knowledge that an audience brings to a concert; it is therefore difficult to estimate the level of technical knowledge you can assume in your writing. You want to avoid overly technical analyses that will make no sense to the majority of the audience. Conversely, the program notes should not insult the audience's intelligence by assuming that they know nothing at all about music. People devote their valuable time and money to attending concerts because of their interest in music. Most members of a concert audience collect classical records and have a fair general knowledge of the history of music. Write for an imaginary nonmusician who is interested in music and is fairly well read. If the program consists of standard works, your imaginary reader probably already knows something about them and may have heard other live or recorded performances of these works. Our imaginary listener appreciates being reminded, or told for the first time, about the special circumstances surrounding the composition of a particular work, the composer's intent, and some idea of what makes the work unique.

The question of which audience to write for may be particularly troublesome when you are writing notes for a recital presented as part of your work toward a music degree. The audience will probably include relatives and friends who are there mainly because they are proud of you, teachers who will judge the recital on technical grounds, and some of your student colleagues, who will bring their special knowledge and background to the experience. In that situation, I would not aim the notes at either your relatives or your teachers, but somewhere in the middle. Since the audience at student recitals usually consists largely of students and faculty members, try to write at a more technical level than would be appropriate for a general concert audience, while avoiding the other extreme of assuming that everyone knows the music as intimately as you and your teacher do.

RESEARCH

Approach the research for program notes in the same way as you approach research for a paper, using the same resources and methodology, beginning with dictionaries and encyclopedias, histories, biographies, and thematic catalogs. It may seem strange to pursue the same sort of research for a few short paragraphs of program notes as for a twenty-page paper, but whatever you write in program notes, no matter how brief, must be based on a thorough understanding of the music, as well as awareness of the background of the work, where it fits in the composer's output, and the composer's intent. In writing program notes, you rarely use all the information uncovered in your research, but it is a serious mistake to toss off a few casual comments without really knowing what you are talking about. If you are performing the work you are writing about, you should have analyzed it already, but you may need to do some research on its background and on the composer's intent. If you do not already know the work thoroughly, then that must be the first step in your research—no one should ever write about a musical work without studying the score, and hearing a recording, if possible. The audience may not realize that the few paragraphs they read are based on hours of careful research, but each sentence you write must be based on thorough knowledge. The world does not need any more vague, fanciful, or flowery program notes; quite enough of that sort of prose has been written already. The process of research into musical topics is explained in Chapter 3.

WORKING WITHIN LIMITS

The main constraint on program notes is always limited space. If you are told that there is room in the program for five hundred words, then you must stay within that limit. If you go over the word limit, you cause endless problems for the people responsible for printing the program. They will either shorten your prose themselves, ask you to do it if there is time, or leave out the notes altogether. If your limit is five hundred words, then everything you say must fit on two pages of double-spaced typescript with normal margins. Every word you write must be carefully chosen. Space limitations are not always that severe, but the writer must stay within whatever limit is imposed.

In some ways, it is more difficult to discuss a piece of music in a paragraph or two than to write a twenty-page paper about it. In a paper, one has the leisure to develop ideas at some length, cite long quotations, and write extended analytical discussions. There is no room in program notes for footnotes; quotations have to be brief and must be chosen with great care. It can be very helpful to quote a composer's words about what he had in mind for a particular work, but quotations must be short and effective. One usually cannot include musical examples, and extended analyses are impossible because of the space limitations. Besides, program notes in the "then this happens, then this happens" style make dull reading. The writer hopes to draw the listener's attention to something interesting or unique about a particular work, and that is about all one can accomplish. Program notes are not research papers, but neither are they collections of vague sentiments about music in general or about a particular composer. Through a kind of sleight of hand, the writer tries to convey a genuine understanding of a particular work in a few well-chosen words.

As you can see, it is a challenging task to write effective program notes. Sometimes, in an attempt to meet a deadline, students resort to copying or paraphrasing material from published collections of program notes or from record jackets. Needless to say, such copying, whether or not it constitutes technical plagiarism, is a serious mistake, just as it would be in a paper. Some published notes and record jackets are written in a flowery style that would be difficult to pass off as your own work, and some have little worthwhile to say about the music. It is clearly better to do your own research, analyze the music, and try to communicate your insight in a clear and informative manner in the short space allotted to you.

SPECIAL PROBLEMS

Some kinds of concerts present special challenges for the writer of program notes. The following brief comments offer general guidelines for writing program notes in these special situations.

Early Music

The music of the medieval, Renaissance, and baroque periods was usually written to be performed in a context far different from today's concert hall. Early music, at least that portion that was written down, was generally performed either in church or in court. Composers and performers worked for the church or the aristocracy and succeeded as long as they continued to provide the kind of music that would satisfy their powerful patrons.

It is often helpful for the audience to be reminded of the special circumstances for which a work was written. Think, for example, of the pieces discussed in Chapter 2. Listeners would be better prepared to appreciate a performance of Dufay's *Nuper rosarum flores* if they knew something of the special circumstances surrounding its purpose and performance. Even if a listener cannot hear the mathematical relationships between the two slow-moving lines, it is helpful to know that Dufay was trying to model his musical structures on the architectural proportions of the new cathedral. At a concert performance of a Bach cantata, the audience should understand that the cantatas were not written as concert pieces, but were integral to the long Sunday morning service of the German Lutheran church.

There are other historical questions that may deserve comment. In the Middle Ages and the Renaissance, and to some extent in the baroque period, composer and performer were the same person, not two different specialists. Music was often written for instruments and vocal groups different from the ones that usually perform the music now. In addition, much of the music of the Middle Ages and the Renaissance was written in a shorthand form, so that performers must reconstruct the musical details rather than following specific directions set down by the composer. Baroque music generally requires substantial ornamentation and filling in of parts written in skeletal fashion. The audience should understand these historical differences in the fundamental relationship between composer and performer, and should be aware of the decisions for which the performers are responsible, as well as the circumstances for which the music was originally written. If modern instruments are substituted for the instruments that the composer intended, that fact should be noted. One need not construct an elaborate defense of the practice, but the listener should at least be aware that using modern instruments may change the sound the composer had in mind. Whatever the writer can convey about the original purpose and sound of the music will help the audience appreciate the performance better and will equip them to make an intelligent judgment about the success of the performers' reconstructive work.

Transcriptions, Arrangements, and Editions

An allied issue is the question of the relationship between what the performers play and what the composer actually wrote. The listener should be told something of the history of a work if he or she is to appreciate the performance. If a particular clavier concerto by Bach, for example, is a transcription of a violin concerto by Vivaldi, the notes should mention that fact. If the score used in a performance is a modern transcription or arrangement of an earlier work, that fact should be noted. Another example from the music of Bach comes to mind. Cellists enjoy performing the so-called gamba sonatas of Bach; these works, however, were transcribed by Bach for solo gamba and harpsichord with an *obbligato* right-hand part, from earlier trio sonatas written for two treble instruments and continuo, in which the harpsichord part consists of a figured bass line. Again, this information is interesting to the intelligent listener. In the same way, modern restorations of the original versions of works from the romantic period, or from any period, should be noted. The audience certainly wants to know whether what they hear is the original work, a "corrected" version by an overly zealous editor, or a modern reconstruction of the original version.

Recent Music

World premieres and recently composed music can pose a difficult problem for the writer of program notes. The usual research resources are of limited use; they may contain useful information about the life of the composer and his place in twentieth-century music, but they do not contain information about recently composed works. If you are writing the notes for your own performance, you can work from your knowledge of the score; if not, it may be difficult to get access to a score. In that case, you must try to contact the composer by mail or in person to find out about the work. Some composers are very helpful in explaining the genesis and the structure of their work. Others dislike discussing their creations and prefer to let their works speak for them. Some composers, when asked about their works, embark on long disquisitions about Oriental philosophy, complex mathematical principles, or antiwar sentiments. Usually, the diligent investigator can find out something of what the composer had in mind and where the work fits in the evolution of twentieth-century musical styles. Any information of this sort is helpful to the listener, who then is saved from the danger of judging the work against a false set of expectations. The composer's ideas may or may not be audible in the performance, but at least the listener knows what to listen for and can judge the work on the grounds of whether it communicates what the composer had in mind.

Overly Familiar Repertory

The writer of program notes faces the opposite problem when writing notes about works everyone knows, like the Beethoven symphonies or some of the better-known late Romantic works. One feels tongue-tied and a bit foolish when trying to write about these works—what can there be left to say about the "Eroica," for example, or the Chopin preludes? The way to approach this situation is exactly the way one approaches any writing about music—research. One can always discuss basic issues like the background of the work, the composer's intent, the structure of the work, or the qualities that make the work unique. Vast amounts of information have been written about the better-known composers and their works, so that in one sense it is easier to find things to say about these works. Published letters of composers may contain information about how the composer thought of the work, the circumstances of the first performance, and the reaction of the audience and the critics. It is easy to find the writings of well-known composers; a carefully chosen quotation may give the reader a new slant on a familiar work.

Texts and Translations

One final issue that should be discussed is the question of providing texts and translations of vocal music. In general, the listener should always be provided with the text, whether the singers will be singing in English or in a foreign language. If the performance will be in a foreign language, the listener should have both the foreign text and an English translation so that he or she can follow the text as it is performed and can check the translation in case he or she does not read the foreign language with facility.

The principle is clear enough, but some situations present special problems. If a text is extremely long or if there are a large number of texts, as in a *Lieder* recital, it may take a large amount of space to reprint both texts and translations. In that case, an insert containing the texts and translations can be folded into the program. Some texts are familiar to most listeners; if a choral group is performing a Renaissance Mass, for example, most members of the audience would know the familiar liturgical texts and what they mean in English. Even in that case, however, programs frequently contain both text and translation. The translations chosen should be as literal as possible so that the members of the audience who are not familiar with the original language can judge the aptness of the musical setting to the individual words of text. If the translator's name is known, it should always be included with the translation, and there may be issues of copyright to deal with. Finally, when you have gone to the trouble of providing texts and translations, make sure that there is enough light in the hall during the performance so that the audience can follow the texts; it makes little sense to provide texts if the hall will be too dark for reading.

CONCLUSION

Writing program notes may be a daunting challenge because of the extreme economy of writing style called for and the special problems posed by unusual repertory. Informative and carefully written program notes, however, are welcomed by intelligent audience members and can add greatly to the listening experience.

chapter 9

Concert Reports

Another type of assignment that involves writing about music is the concert report. Generally, when professors assign reports, they make their expectations clear, but there still are a few generalizations we can make about this kind of assignment.

PURPOSE

While each instructor may have his or her own goals in assigning concert reports, most instructors see these reports as extensions of the classroom discussions. Concert reports are an example of what psychologists call second-order learning—applying theoretical information and insight to new experiences. It is one thing to absorb what an instructor says in class and be able to repeat it in an examination; it is another thing altogether to have such command of the analytical methods and stylistic insights discussed in class that one can use them as a guide to judging a new musical experience.

The focus of a concert report should therefore be *musical style*. Too many concert reports waste a great deal of time discussing issues that have nothing to do with musical style—descriptions of the hall, the audience, the appearance of the performers, or the technical success of the performance. Concert reports should not be critical pieces. Music criticism, a combination of scholarly writing and journalism, may involve the same sort of research as a paper or program notes, but it also involves a number of other goals and is bound by the same general rules and time pressures as other kinds of journalistic writing.

Questions of performance practice may relate to the question of musical style. Discussion of the quality of the performance, however, can easily degenerate into criticism of the playing or comments about problems of ensemble coordination, intonation, and the like.

What instructors want to see in concert reports is discussion of the music in terms of the stylistic issues discussed in class. Classes studying baroque music, for example, are frequently asked to attend concerts in which music composed before 1750 is performed and to discuss what they hear in terms of the stylistic developments discussed in class. Comparisons with examples discussed in class are welcome. Discussion of performance practice issues is also welcome; instructors expect that the students will apply the information they have learned in class to all musical experiences in the future.

RESEARCH

It sometimes surprises students to find out that they might have to do some research before attending a concert about which they plan to write a report. Obviously, you will be better prepared to deal with the stylistic issues involved in a performance if you learn what you can about the work before hearing it performed. If the listener goes to the concert armed with an understanding of where this particular work fits in the evolution of musical style, he or she will be in a much better position to discuss the work from a stylistic viewpoint and to judge whether the performance was stylistically valid. It is lack of preparation, or lack of advance understanding of what a work is about, that causes students to resort to comments on irrelevant issues like the dress or deportment of performers or audiences.

Finally, the major thing to keep in the forefront of your mind as you draft your concert report is *musical style*. If you focus on stylistic issues, then you are demonstrating to your instructor that you have thought about the issues discussed in class and that you can discuss stylistic questions competently and intelligently.

chapter 10

Essay Examinations

There is one final type of writing about music that is very much part of your life as a student—writing essay questions about music in examinations. Reading a large number of essay questions is often a discouraging task; few people produce effective prose under the pressure that surrounds an important examination. The answers usually vary enormously in quality, from unorganized facts scrawled in incomplete and awkward sentences to the occasional well-organized and convincing essay. Knowing how to approach writing essay questions can materially affect your grades and therefore your academic success. This chapter will discuss the purpose of essay questions, how to prepare for them, the steps to follow in writing a successful essay as part of an examination, and some common errors with which students defeat themselves in this type of examination.

PURPOSE

Professors do not include essay questions in their examinations to be cruel or because of the pleasure they derive from reading the essays. Essay questions are important because they provide an opportunity for students to demonstrate their grasp of important material and because they call for insight, understanding, and the ability to synthesize large amounts of information and focus on the most significant material. Life is not multiple-choice. To ask only objective or short-answer questions is to do a severe injustice to the material, since the history of music is not a series of unrelated facts and details. Essay questions are the only way to test the student's grasp of the big picture, as well as important trends and connections.

PREPARING FOR ESSAY EXAMINATIONS

One of the important advantages of essay questions, from the instructor's point of view, is that preparing for essay questions gives shape and coherence to the process of reviewing the material. Preparing for the examination thus becomes an important part of the learning experience, not simply an exercise in memorizing facts

There are several steps involved in preparing for essay questions. First of all, you must know in advance if there will be essay questions on the examination. If you know essay questions will be asked, during your review make a list of those areas that you think are particularly important or that were given special emphasis by the instructor. If you pick out five or six areas that you think are the obvious choices for essay questions, you can guarantee that one or more of those questions will appear in some form on the examination. After all, professors emphasize areas that they think are particularly important, and it would be pointless to ask essay questions about side issues or unimportant details. If you go over your notes with an eye to those areas that the professor emphasized, you can write the questions in advance and plan your answers. You can even design outlines for the answers to the questions you think are the most likely to appear on the examination so that your answers will be logical, coherent, and organized.

HOW TO PROCEED

The main trick to writing successful essays in an examination is to *pause and think before you start writing*. That is difficult to do; students usually approach major examinations in a state of nervousness, their minds bulging with recently reviewed facts, anxious to write as much as they can as quickly as possible before they forget everything. Working quickly and impulsively may be the best way to approach objective questions, but it is *not* the way to answer essay questions.

The first thing to do is to read the question a second time and be sure that you understand it. Ask the instructor if you are not sure what the question means. Look for key words—is the idea to trace the important stages in the evolution of a particular style, to discuss a particular work as an example of a particular style, or to compare and contrast two works or two composers? There is a limited number of kinds of essay questions, and professors try very hard to frame essay questions as clearly as possible. The next thing to do is to pause and *think* about the question. What is included? What is not? Are there terms that need defining as the first step? Are there limits set in the question?

The next step is to *outline* your answer and tinker with the outline for a while. Maybe your answer would make better sense if you changed the order of ideas, or perhaps there is something in your outline that you would like to discuss but that does not really fit with the question. It is even possible that you may have acquired some knowledge that you will have no opportunity to demonstrate. It is better to answer the question briefly and stay on the point than to write brilliantly about some other topic.

After you are satisfied that your outline adequately covers the area specified by the question and that you have not left out anything important or included something that does not belong in your discussion, *then* start writing your answer. If there is time, write a rough draft and edit it before you copy your final version. Stay on the point, and force yourself to follow your outline in a coherent fashion. Avoid the tendency to spew out unrelated facts, and do your best to produce a piece of writing that flows logically and coherently. Finally, assuming there is time, edit and proofread your answer, make sure it is legible, and cross out anything that is ungrammatical, incoherent, or not relevant to the question. Remember that your aim is to demonstrate understanding, insight, and a command of large questions, not to produce a long list of unrelated facts. Remember that your professor will have to read a large stack of examinations. After a few hours of grading papers, it is a pleasure to encounter a clearly organized and carefully written essay. A coherent and careful piece of writing will be much more successful than a sloppy, rambling, disorganized scrawl, even if the two contain the same information. The trick is to *organize* the information, not just regurgitate it.

COMMON ERRORS

The usual mistakes that students make when writing essay examinations are easily avoidable. The main mistake is not to read the question carefully or not to read the instructions. When some students read a question, one key word triggers a flood of facts that may not be relevant to that question. If the question, for example, asks you to contrast the styles of French baroque and Venetian opera, do not launch into a long description of Lully's life and career, even though he is an important figure in French baroque opera. Focus on exactly what the question asks for. If the question is "Trace the evolution of the motet from Notre Dame polyphony through the French Ars Nova," leave out the English school, no matter how well prepared you are to write about Dunstable's motets. If the question is "Discuss *The Rake's Progress* as an example of Stravinsky's neoclassical style," do not ramble on about the Octet for Winds, even if you know much more about it than you do about the opera or think it is a better example of neoclassicism than *The Rake's Progress*. Although it seems obvious that the key to success is to answer the question posed by the instructor rather than writing about something else that you like better, time and again students wander off into areas specifically excluded by the professor's carefully written question.

The other major failing with most answers to essay questions is that students produce an unorganized jumble of facts more or less related to the question, rather than a thoughtful, coherent essay. Many students seem to think that their task is to put down everything they can think of, leaving it to the instructor to pick out what he or she wants. Everything important is in there somewhere, if the instructor is willing to dig for it and if he or she does not care about the order in which things appear. That approach is distressingly common and may be a result of the overemphasis on isolated facts in some of our music history books, as well as in our educational system in general. This tendency may also be a result of the television age, with its emphasis on short bursts of information, or of the nervousness with which students approach examinations. I cannot overemphasize the importance of logical organization and coherence. If you approach essay questions in the way just outlined, you will succeed—it's that simple.

The last common error is to fail to proofread and edit your essay. The professor will never know how well you have answered the question if he or she cannot read what you have written. Be sure everything is legible, copy the essay over if it is a mess, change as many misspellings and grammatical errors as you can in the remaining time, and make the essay look as competent and professional as you can, granting the pressures of the examination situation.

CONCLUSION

Remember that the object of essay questions is not to produce a reflex response or a bit of information, but to organize large amounts of information, selecting the most significant events and trends relevant to the question and organizing them in a logical fashion. Essay questions are a test of understanding and insight, not a test of whether you have memorized a sufficient number of bits of information. Logic, coherence, and clear writing will be much more successful than covering several pages with hastily scrawled facts.

chapter 11

Principles of Style

Chapters 11–14 present some basic ideas about writing effective prose. Since you have had courses in writing in the past, much of this material will be a review for you rather than new information. Many books on writing treat these matters in much more detail; this section is intended only as a review, included here for your convenience. Although some of this discussion applies to any expository writing, we will also discuss the problems peculiar to papers on musical topics. This first chapter will review some general principles. Subsequent chapters will deal with details of effective writing style and common problems that detract from the effectiveness of student papers.

DIFFERENT KINDS OF PROSE

Expository prose is different from much of the writing we see each day, because it is designed to inform and explain. Other kinds of writing have different purposes. Advertising copy, for example, is often designed not to convey information but to create an aura of pleasant associations around a product; such prose often speaks to our emotions rather than to our minds. When an advertisement speaks of "a totally unique and surprisingly afford-able driving experience, comparable to the best European road cars," the writer is not appealing to our minds. If he stated plainly that this car is cheaper than a Mercedes, but just as good, we would not believe him. Instead, he is trying to make us feel good about the car.

Sometimes prose is written to mask or sanitize unpleasant ideas, through what is called euphemism. When a politician speaks of "revenue enhancement strategies" instead of "raising taxes," he or she is trying to hide the real meaning from outraged voters. After the Challenger disaster, a NASA spokesman, speaking to the shocked world, referred to the remains of those killed in the explosion as "recovered components" and called the coffins in which those remains were shipped home "crew transfer containers."

Frequently, prose is written to create a favorable impression of the writer rather than to explain ideas or content. When academic committees speak of "curriculum evaluation criteria" or "recruitment strategies for the modern multiversity," their aim is not to communicate ideas but to create an impression of importance and seriousness. When a businessman speaks of "ballpark projections on the downside effects of targeting our marketing to new demographics," he, too, is creating an impression, attempting to convince his colleagues that his judgments are based on sophisticated business sense. Read the prose that comes your way with a critical eye, and ask yourself what the writer's purpose is. Once you understand the purpose of expository prose, as opposed to the aims of other kinds of prose, you will better understand the tone and style appropriate for it.

TONE

Since the purpose of expository prose is to inform and explain, its main goal is clarity. Your goal in a paper about music is to convey complex ideas about a complicated art as clearly and directly as possible. The focus should be on communicating concepts, not on convincing the reader that you are an expert. Your prose therefore should be as direct and as simple as you can make it, so that the reader is informed and enlightened.

The tone of your writing should be crisp, professional, and businesslike. That is not to say that you should avoid using technical terms. Like the jargon of all fields, the technical terms of music exist because we need them. There is no other economical way to communicate a concept like "fugue" or "sonata-allegro structure"; the technical terms convey precise information to the musically informed reader. As to the rest of your language, however, clarity and crispness of expression is the goal.

Two extremes are to be avoided. Expository prose is different from both speech and informal writing, such as personal letters. A slangy or cute tone is therefore completely out of place in a formal paper. Sometimes student papers contain sentences like "Well! You can imagine my surprise when I found that..." or "His solution to the problem is totally radical." Such language is embarrassing in a formal paper.

A more common error in student papers is to go to the other extreme and adopt a stilted, artificial style. Students sometimes use awkward impersonal constructions like "It has long been assumed that..." and "The present writer finds it well-nigh impossible to agree with this position." Sometimes the writing becomes overly dramatic, like the following example.

> When Josquin entered the service of the Duke as a young choirboy, little did the world suspect that in the future he would have such a profound impact on the history of Renaissance music.

Perhaps stilted or flowery language appeals to some students because they think it creates an impression of serious scholarship or because it feels safe to hide behind impersonal language.

The proper tone for expository writing is somewhere between these two extremes. The first priority should always be *clarity.* Individual concepts must be explained as clearly as possible, the ideas must be set forth in a unified and coherent way, and the argument must flow logically so that the reader can follow the line of your logic. Your writing should be clear, crisp, economical, businesslike, and professional.

THE STANCE OF THE WRITER

Related to the question of tone is the issue of the writer's stance, or how involved the person of the writer should be in the prose. Again, there are two extremes to avoid.

The first extreme is for the writer to be too intrusive. Some students write with a tone of breathless discovery, as if no one had ever considered these ideas or heard this music before. This approach tells the reader more about the naiveté of the writer than anything useful about the topic.

The other extreme is the elusive or invisible writer. As I explained earlier, research means more than merely reporting the ideas of others. The researcher is expected to design a hypothesis, study the evidence, review the secondary literature, analyze the music, and then form his or her own conclusions, based on critical judgment and analytical ability. The writer is expected to take a stand and communicate his or her opinions. After the writer cites expert A and expert B, the reader waits for the other shoe to drop—what does the writer think? To stay aloof from your prose, reluctant to share your conclusions, is to shirk one of the fundamental responsibilities of the researcher.

THE QUESTION OF PRONOUNS

The question of the writer's stance brings up the question of how the writer should refer to himself or herself. Many of us were trained to avoid the first person pronoun in our writing and find it difficult to write *I* in a paper.

Different professors have different ideas about this question; many agree that *I* is perfectly acceptable, provided that it is used with restraint and reserved for those moments when the writer is sharing his or her own thoughts. Clearly, *I* is out of place when discussing someone else's ideas, but there are few alternatives to *I* when it comes to the writer's own conclusions. "The present writer" is an awkward and distracting phrase. *I* seems much more natural in a sentence like "A says this and B says that; I agree with B." One can, of course, avoid pronouns altogether by writing something like "A says this, B says that; considering all the evidence, B's position seems more valid."

I is not the appropriate pronoun to use in a general statement that any informed reader would agree with. Consider the following sentences.

As I look at the number of cantatas Bach composed in his first few years at Leipzig, I am astounded.
As we look at the number of cantatas . . ., we are astounded.
As one looks at the number of cantatas . . ., one is astounded.

The first version, using *I*, seems arrogant. The chronology of Bach's cantatas is fairly common knowledge and has been in print for years; emphasizing your personal astonishment simply points out that you have come upon the information only recently. Both *we* and *one* are adequate for sentences like this. Some writers are uncomfortable with *one*, feeling that it is a stiff or old-fashioned construction, but it works well in general statements of this sort. If choosing a pronoun makes you uncomfortable, find another way to write the sentence—one can always find another way to say almost anything. In this case, you can avoid using any pronouns by reworking the sentence.

The number of cantatas composed by Bach . . . is astounding.

In summary, use *I* when the idea is really yours, when you are sharing your own views, and when you are stating your conclusions, based on your research and analysis. Use other pronouns when you are making more general statements. "The present writer" should be relegated to the dustbin with other phrases no longer in use.

chapter 12

Writing Effective Sentences

The act of writing, whether the work is expository prose, fiction, or poetry, consists of choosing and assembling the words that will convey one's ideas as effectively as possible. The writer's responsibility boils down to choosing the next word, just as the composer's task ultimately consists of deciding what the next note should be. Our discussion of writing style thus must begin at the basic level of choosing appropriate words. This chapter will then move on to a discussion of good and bad combinations of words and to questions of sentence structure.

WORD CHOICE

The basic work of writing is the selection of appropriate words to convey the idea you have in mind. Care and precision in choosing the right words is what makes the difference between a convincing paper and one that is weak and boring. There are a few general principles that will help you make appropriate choices.

First, bear in mind that the English language, because of its long and involved history, is much richer in vocabulary and synonyms than most other languages. Over the centuries, English has adopted words from Anglo-Saxon, Norman French, Greek, Latin, French, Spanish, Italian, Arabic, and a host of other languages. You therefore have at your disposal an incredible wealth of synonyms for any word or idea, each with its own particular flavor and force. Browsing through a dictionary or a thesaurus gives one a sense of the huge English vocabulary; most of us use only a small fraction of the words available to us.

The huge vocabulary of modern English means that the writer has no reason to settle for awkward or inappropriate words. We turn now to some specific recommendations about word choice.

Slang

Use words in their original senses; avoid any slang usage that is different from a word's standard sense. As you know, slang changes rapidly. As soon as the general population adopts a colorful slang usage, the group that originated the slang phrase stops using it and invents new phrases that will keep their language private. In a formal paper, avoid using normal words in their slang senses, and, of course, avoid words that exist only in slang. Even the slang words that are acceptable in some areas of the musical world, like "bone" for "trombone," or "fiddle" for "violin," should not be used in formal papers.

Anglo-Saxon and Latin Roots

Words derived from Anglo-Saxon roots are usually shorter, more concrete, and more forceful than words derived from Latin roots. "Church music" is more forceful than "ecclesiastical music"; "went mad" is stronger than "suffered a complete personality disintegration." You cannot avoid Latin roots altogether, any more than you can avoid technical terms, but you should always stop to consider whether you can find a simpler, livelier way to say what you want to say.

Foreign Words

Foreign words may sometimes be unavoidable in your prose. Since many foreign words have no exact equivalent in English, using a foreign term may be the best way, or the only way, to say exactly what you want to say. It is a mistake, however, to use foreign words just for effect. The constant use of foreign words gives your prose a stuffy and pedantic flavor and creates the impression that you are more interested in showing off your erudition than in communicating your ideas. Consider the following sentence.

The *Weltanschauung* underlying the early songs is in keeping with the *Zeitgeist* of *fin-de-siècle* Vienna.

That sentence sounds pretentious. You can say the same thing using standard English words, or decide to keep one of the foreign terms, perhaps *fin-de-siècle* because it conveys more than the usual English translation, "turn-of-the-century."

Use Words Literally

Respect the literal force of words and use them in the way the world at large uses them. *Unique,* for example, means "the only one in the world." To describe something as "somewhat unique" or "totally unique" is meaningless; it is impossible to be somewhat unique, just as it is impossible to be somewhat pregnant. *Hopefully* means "in a spirit of hope," not "I hope that." Thus a sentence like "Hopefully, we will hear more authentic performances in the future" makes no sense. Lately, *decimate* seems to be used as a synonym for *devastate,* in sentences like "The town was decimated by the flood." *Decimate,* from the Latin *decima* ("tenth"), means to destroy ten percent of something. We could go on with other examples, but the point is clear—respect the literal meaning of the words you use.

Creating New Words

Use existing words; there is no reason to create new words by piling prefixes or suffixes onto existing words. In modern English, there is a tendency to tack *-ize* or *-wise* onto almost any word. The resulting neologisms, such as *prioritize, finalize,* and *background-wise,* are ugly and unnecessary. The writer should be able to find a respectable English word or phrase that will convey the idea gracefully. Sometimes music students create awkward hybrids like "analyzation," "texture-wise," and "a minuet-type movement." Take the trouble to find the appropriate word from the rich vocabulary of standard English, and do not resort to artificial and ungainly creations.

Nouns Are Nouns and Verbs Are Verbs

Use words as their proper parts of speech. There is a tendency in some areas of modern English to make nouns out of verbs, verbs out of nouns, adjectives out of nouns or verbs, and so forth. "All systems are definitely in a go configuration" may be fashionable at NASA headquarters, but it is unacceptable in a paper. In standard English, *access* is a noun, not a verb; "I was unable to access the primary sources" might sound normal in a computer science class, but that usage is not acceptable in a formal paper.

WORD COMBINATIONS

Variety of Word Choice

It is not enough to choose the right individual word; sometimes a perfectly appropriate word becomes inappropriate in context because it already appears in the previous phrase. Consider the following sentence.

Works by twenty-five composers appear in this collection of works, and the fact that there are no weak works speaks highly of the work of these composers.

That sentence is ungainly because of the repetition of *works* or *work*. It can easily be repaired by using synonyms and doing some judicious cutting.

Works by twenty-five composers appear in the collection, and the fact that there are no weak pieces speaks highly of the skill of these composers.

This issue is complicated further when one writes about music, because one must avoid using words that become technical terms in the musical context. Words like *key, major, minor, development,* and so forth cannot be used both as general words and as special musical terms. Sentences like the following cause confusion.

The key element in sonata-allegro structure is the element of key.
One of the major developments in the romantic symphony is the emphasis on the development sections.

These sentences can easily be rewritten, keeping the musical terms as technical terms and finding synonyms for those words when they are used in a nonmusical sense.

The determining factor in sonata-allegro structure is the element of key.
One important change in the romantic symphony is the new emphasis on development sections.

Noun Strings

There is a tendency in modern English to create phrases out of strings of loosely related nouns. We have already mentioned phrases like "revenue enhancement strategies" and "curriculum evaluation criteria." In papers on music, one sees phrases like "the composer-control issue" and "the patron-composer relationship." The hyphen does not solve the problem; those phrases are still strings of vaguely related nouns, not correct English phrases. Standard English would say "the issue of the composer's control" and "the relationship between patron and composer," or something similar.

Redundant Couplets

In modern English one frequently sees the combination of an adjective and a noun, the two meaning the same thing. Common examples are "general consensus," "subject matter," and "end result." In each case, one of the words is unnecessary padding. A common redundant couplet in papers about music is "in-depth analysis," a pretentious and ugly wording. First, *in-depth* is a stale catch phrase; it is also an artificial adjective constructed by jamming together a preposition and its object. Second, it is redundant; *all* analysis is "in-depth," since analysis means breaking a phenomenon down into its parts and studying each in detail. Avoid redundant prefixes, also, in creations like *interrelationship. Inter*, a Latin borrowing, means "between"; since all relationships must be between two or more entities, the prefix is redundant.

Stock Couplets

Stock couplets are combinations of adjectives and nouns that always seem to appear together. "Abject poverty," "utter despair," "reckless abandon," and "extenuating circumstances" are common examples. By now, *extenuating* seems to have lost its meaning, having become an appendage attached for reasons of rhythm to the word *circumstances.* One student's concert report contained the following sentence.

Unfortunately the first piece listed on the program was not performed because of extenuating circumstances.

I assume that the student meant "unforeseen" or "unavoidable" circumstances. Try to avoid stock couplets because of the flabbiness of these overused phrases. In descriptions of music, find alternatives for such stock phrases as "lyrical second theme" and "dramatic opening gesture."

The "Not un-" Construction

Avoid the pretentious "not un-" construction, as in "It was not uncommon in the Renaissance for composers to begin their careers as choirboys in the chapels of the great courts." That construction is weak and affected, and overuse of it rapidly becomes not unannoying.

Dependence on Modifiers

In general, rely on strong nouns and verbs rather than modifiers to convey your ideas. One way to tighten up your writing is to eliminate all qualifying adverbs like *somewhat, virtually, literally, perhaps,* and *very.* If the nouns and verbs have been chosen with care, qualifiers rarely add anything to the sentence; in fact, they weaken the force of your writing. The reason that we tend to rely so much on modifiers is that many of the words we use constantly have lost their force. "A brilliant performance" sounds like high praise, but if you regularly use that adjective to describe any performance in which the players manage to end more or less together, then you have to find something stronger, like "exceptionally brilliant," to describe a superior performance. If everyone who has ever set foot on a stage, appeared in a film, or made a recording is called a "star," then exceptional performers have to be classified as "superstars." Once that term has been cheapened through indiscriminate use, we will need still another category—perhaps "megastar" or "demigod." If you choose strong, colorful nouns and verbs, you will not need to tack a modifier onto every word. Since you will need fewer words to convey your ideas, your writing will automatically become more forceful and effective.

SENTENCE STRUCTURE

Writing effective expository prose is not simply a matter of choosing the right words. No matter how appropriate each word is, your prose can still turn out to be boring or difficult to understand, depending on how you deal with the matter of sentence structure.

Passive Voice

One kind of sentence structure that frequently weakens student prose is the passive voice. Some students seem to feel that constructions based on the passive voice are appropriate, or perhaps required, in scholarly writing. The passive voice is occasionally acceptable, but as a general rule, one should avoid it. Particularly weak are awkward impersonal constructions, like the following:

It has often been stated...

In this study, several examples of the Baroque *concerto grosso* have been analyzed...

Vivaldi has frequently been viewed as...

In each of the preceding sentences, the language is vague, awkward, and indefinite, and seems to hint at vast stores of knowledge that the writer is not willing to share. The reader wonders about the missing subjects—*who* has often stated this, viewed Vivaldi in this way, or analyzed these concerti? The active voice, with a clear subject, verb, and object, is always better than the passive voice. Avoid those impersonal "it" constructions altogether.

Word Order

Since English grammar depends on word order rather than on inflected endings to indicate the case of nouns, changing the word order changes the meaning you convey in both gross and subtle ways. Consider the different force and emphasis of the following sentences.

After the large-scale works of his early period, Stravinsky turned to a new idiom, the neoclassical style, which represents his chief contribution to twentieth-century music.

After the large-scale works of his early period, which represent his chief contribution to twentieth-century music, Stravinsky turned to a new idiom, the neoclassical style.

Stravinsky turned to a new idiom, the neoclassical style, which represents his chief contribution to twentieth-century music, after the large-scale works of his early period.

After the large-scale works of his early period, Stravinsky turned to a new idiom, his chief contribution to twentieth-century style—neoclassicsm.

The first sentence is perfectly clear, and the word order is acceptable. The second version, by putting the subordinate clause after "period" rather than "idiom," makes nonsense of the sentence, or at least materially changes its sense. The third version is correct but weak, since after making its point, the sentence trails off with a relatively unimportant adverbial phrase. The fourth version is the strongest, since it puts the important term, neoclassicism, in the strong final position. When you edit your work, try changing the order of elements in your sentences until the words not only say what you want to say, but also say it with the exact shade of emphasis that you intend.

Parallel Ideas

When you want to emphasize the relationship between parallel elements of a sentence, or the contrast between them, keep the sentence structures parallel. Consider the following sentence.

Among the most typical examples of the symphonic poem are *Les Préludes* and *Orpheus* by Liszt; another example is Smetana's *Má Vlast.*

The problem with that sentence is that Smetana seems to be added as an afterthought. The reader wonders exactly what the writer meant to say. The idea is much clearer when the series is kept in parallel construction.

Among the most typical examples of the symphonic poem are *Les Préludes* and *Orpheus* by Liszt and *Má Vlast* by Smetana.

Parallel construction is also the clearest way to emphasize the contrast between two ideas. Compare the following sentences.

Bach, a church musician, composed cantatas and Passions; Handel specialized in opera and oratorio, since he worked for the English court.

Bach, a church musician, composed cantatas and Passions; Handel, a court musician, composed operas and oratorios.

The second sentence, with its parallel structure, emphasizes the contrast between the two composers much more strongly than the first sentence.

Variety of Sentence Structure

Just as well-chosen words will not produce effective prose if sentence structure is not handled correctly, individually correct sentences do not result in effective paragraphs unless there is variety in the sentence structure. A series of short, subject-verb-object sentences creates a choppy and childish effect; a string of long, involved sentences makes it unduly difficult for the reader to follow your thought. Since any structure becomes tiresome when it turns into an invariable pattern, one key to effective writing is to vary the sentence structure. Consider the following paragraphs.

William Byrd was born in Lincolnshire in 1543. He studied with Thomas Tallis. He was appointed organist of Lincoln Cathedral in 1568. He was elected a member of the Chapel Royal in 1570.

William Byrd was born, probably in Lincolnshire, although the documentary proof of this fact is less than definitive, in 1543. It is commonly assumed, in the absence of incontrovertible proof, that he studied music with Thomas Tallis, another organist, Gentleman of the Chapel Royal under several English monarchs, and co-holder, with Byrd, of a royal patent for the publication of music, although that of course did not occur until much later, after Byrd had begun his career as an organist and been himself elected to the post of Gentleman of the Chapel Royal, while still retaining his organ position, at least for some years.

The style of the first paragraph is choppy and childish. The second is just the opposite. By the time the reader finishes that second rambling sentence, with all its afterthoughts, qualifiers, and digressions, he or she no longer knows or cares who the original subject was. When your syntax gets that tangled, you need to stop and think about exactly what you want to say. Much of that material should be eliminated, and the syntax should be greatly simplified.

Remember, also, that complex sentences, with some ideas subordinated, are generally clearer and stronger than compound sentences, which treat all the ideas as equal in importance. Compare the following sentences.

Byrd studied music with Thomas Tallis, then he was appointed organist of Lincoln Cathedral, and shortly thereafter he was elected a Gentleman of the Chapel Royal.

After he studied music with Thomas Tallis and served as organist of Lincoln Cathedral, Byrd was elected a Gentleman of the Chapel Royal in 1570.

The first sentence treats the three events as equal and falls into a breathless and childish style. The second puts the emphasis on Byrd's appointment to the Chapel Royal and subordinates the other events.

By now you can see why the process of writing and editing takes time. The struggle to find exactly the right word and exactly the right grammatical structure to convey what you want to say, with the proper emphasis, takes time and effort. Once you have a series of good sentences, you also must worry about variety of sentence structure. Whenever the structure of a sentence is confusing, back away for a moment and focus on exactly what you are trying to say. Once your *ideas* are clear, you should be able to find *language* that will convey them clearly and effectively.

chapter 13

Effective Paragraphs and the Effective Essay

Just as well-chosen words need to be assembled into well-crafted sentences, so well-written sentences will not convey your thoughts effectively unless they are assembled into well-designed paragraphs and those paragraphs are assembled into a coherent, convincing essay. This chapter will deal with questions of writing style at the larger levels of the paragraph and the essay.

EFFECTIVE PARAGRAPHS

A paragraph is a unified and coherent exposition or explanation of a single idea. A paragraph should constitute a unit of thought, and the chief quality it must have is coherence. The paragraph needs a topic sentence that states the single idea that the paragraph will develop. The rest of the paragraph must be closely related to that single idea. When you are editing your prose, check the paragraphs for unity. If there is anything in a paragraph that does not relate closely to the topic sentence, eliminate the unrelated material or move it somewhere else where it does fit. If a paragraph begins by discussing one idea and then moves into discussion of another idea, make a second paragraph with its own topic sentence out of that material. Read through the following paragraph.

Mahler's Second Symphony, also known as the *Resurrection Symphony*, is one of his best-known works. Like Beethoven, Mahler brings in voices for the final climactic section of the work. After a long, agitated, and highly developed first movement, there follows an Andante in the easy, folksong-like rhythm of an Austrian *Ländler.* The third movement is a symphonic adaptation of one of the *Wunderhorn* songs, and the brief fourth movement is a new setting, for contralto solo, of still another poem from this collection. The finale, after a vivid orchestral section depicting the day of Resurrection, leads to a monumental setting for soloists and chorus of a Resurrection ode by the eighteenth-century German poet, Klopstock. This finale is reminiscent of the Part II of the Eighth Symphony, a monumental movement for soloists and chorus which nearly constitutes a complete secular oratorio, comparable to Liszt's *Faust Symphony,* his oratorio *St. Elizabeth,* or Wagner's *Parsifal.*

The errors in this paragraph should be obvious. Chapter 12 discussed ungainly expressions like "folksong-like"; here our concern is coherence. After a brief description of each of the movements of the Second Symphony, the author suddenly wanders off into a discussion of Part II of the Eighth Symphony. The similarity of the Second and Eighth symphonies deserves brief mention, like the earlier reference to Beethoven, but the last sentence goes far beyond brief mention. By introducing the notion of a secular oratorio and making comparisons to a program symphony, a religious oratorio, and an opera, the writer has let the digression go too far. The last sentence is filled with complex ideas that call for much more explanation and justification than the writer provides, and the reader is distracted from the topic of Mahler's Second Symphony. That last sentence should be shortened considerably, and the writer should eliminate the discussion of the finale of the Eighth Symphony. One of the major tasks of the editing process is "cutting and pasting," literally or figuratively—moving sentences and ideas from paragraph to paragraph or section to section, so that each paragraph is a logical and coherent unit and all the material relevant to each point is grouped in one place.

THE EFFECTIVE ESSAY

Just as a sentence is more than a series of well-chosen words and a paragraph is more than a series of well-constructed sentences, the essay is more than a chain of unified and coherent paragraphs. In Chapter 4, in the section on outlining a paper, some of these ideas were discussed; here our concern is to understand the qualities an essay should have.

A series of paragraphs related to a single topic does not constitute a good essay. The paragraphs must be connected in such a way that the argument moves along logically and coherently. The order in which ideas are presented makes a difference in the effectiveness of the essay as a whole. The entire essay, like each paragraph, must have a topic sentence, and that central theme will determine which paragraphs should be included and which should be cut, as well as suggesting the order in which the material should be discussed.

In the process of turning a series of paragraphs into a coherent essay, the writer needs to add some material to create the large-scale unity and coherence that the essay must have.

Introduction

An essay cannot begin with the first paragraph of the main body of discussion. The essay needs an introduction that will lead into the topic, state the main thesis of the essay, and outline for the reader how the essay will proceed and what kinds of argumentation will be used. Introductions often begin with a general statement, move to the particular area the essay will discuss, and then state the thesis that the essay will defend.

A good introduction avoids two extremes. It is wrong to start abruptly, so that the reader has no chance to see what you plan to do and where your topic fits in the larger view of the history of music. It is also wrong to get carried away with your introductory ideas, so that the introduction becomes a separate, independent essay or introduces ideas and arguments that will not be taken up later in the essay. The introduction should occupy no more than one-tenth of the essay, unless, of course, a longer introduction is necessary to clarify concepts or terms that are essential to your argument.

Transitions

It is critical that the reader of an essay know at all times where he or she is in the course of the argument and where this particular material fits in the overall discussion. Therefore, it is often necessary to add transitional material as you move from one topic to another. The reader has to be aware of where the introduction ends and the main body of the paper begins; he or she also must be made aware when you are moving from one subtopic in the body of the paper to another. Transitions need not be elaborate or long; it is not enough, however, to simply jump from one argument to another. Paragraphs and ideas are not connected into a unified argument by simple proximity; they need to be connected gracefully. The relationship between sections and the reader's position in the logical chain of argumentation must be clear at all times.

Conclusion

An essay of any length must be summarized in a concluding section. If the essay trails off with the last paragraph of argumentation, the reader is left with a feeling of incompleteness and with the task of gathering all the detailed exposition he or she has read into a single, coherent whole. The conclusion need not be as long as the introduction and need not be world-shaking. Some sort of closure, however, is necessary.

One can understand the necessity for a concluding section by analogy with musical structure. The longer a composer has sustained tension and suspense in a piece, the longer the resolution of that suspense needs to be. The short and simple codas appended to classical symphonic movements would never suffice to conclude the longer and more dramatic movements of the romantic period. When you move from short paragraphs to an essay of ten or twenty or thirty pages, the reader needs a proportionately longer introduction and conclusion in order to tie all the ideas together into a coherent statement.

One final warning about writing style in concluding sections. The conclusion should be written in the same tone and style as the rest of the essay. Since conclusions are very difficult to write, students sometimes adopt a hortatory or flowery tone that is inconsistent with the tone and style of the rest of the essay. Remember that the purpose of expository prose is to inform and explain, not to preach, urge the audience to action, or dramatize. Maintain the same competent, informed, and professional tone as the rest of the essay, and bring your work to a clear and forceful close.

CONCLUSION

Each level of writing—the individual word, the sentence, the paragraph, and the essay—has its own stylistic demands and requires the writer's careful attention. At every stage of producing a paper—planning, drafting, and editing—the writer must be attentive to the different demands of each level. Careful and varied sentence structure, coherent and unified paragraphs, and a clearly organized essay, with a helpful introduction, transitions, and conclusions, are just as important as the choice of individual words. Carelessness at any of these levels can defeat the purpose of your work and work against the care and precision exercised at the other levels. An effective prose style results from the writer's understanding of the challenges present at each of these levels and his or her success at meeting those challenges.

chapter 14

Common Writing Problems

This chapter will discuss problems in writing style that appear frequently in student papers, both general writing problems and the special problems that plague students when they write about music. These problems may seem elementary to some readers, but all these mistakes occur frequently in student papers at both the undergraduate and the graduate levels. I have included only the most basic and common problems, based on my experience reading student prose. The standard guides to writing style, such as the *Chicago Manual of Style* or the *Simon & Schuster Handbook for Writers,* contain much more detailed advice on writing correctly and precisely. We will deal first with basic writing errors, and then with the special problems connected with writing about music.

ERRORS IN BASIC WRITING STYLE

Incomplete Sentences

To constitute a complete sentence, a group of words must have at least a subject and a predicate. Some student papers contain incomplete sentences like the following.

Byrd, after studying with Thomas Tallis, a Gentleman of the Chapel Royal, being appointed a cathedral organist, and later winning a position as a court composer.

Impressionism can be understood as an extension of the late romantic aesthetic, expressed through new musical means. Likewise with expressionism.

These examples represent the two situations in which incomplete sentences or "sentence fragments" usually occur. The first consists of the subject followed by a long subordinate clause or string of participial phrases. The writer forgets that he or she has left the subject dangling without a main verb. The second example adds a shorthand afterthought as a separate unit after a perfectly good sentence. This sort of construction is common in spoken style, but it will not pass muster in a formal paper. The second idea must be rewritten as a complete sentence.

Run-on Sentences

The opposite error is to jam too many subjects and verbs into the same sentence, without the proper punctuation or conjunction necessary to separate the complete sentences or clauses.

Ockeghem wrote extremely long lines, with widely spaced cadences and no clear phrase structure, Josquin constructed lines that have a much clearer phrase structure and regularly occurring cadences.

What is written as one long sentence is actually two complete sentences, and the comma is not sufficient punctuation to separate them. This sort of construction often appears with an adverb like *however* or *yet* after the comma. Even with the adverb, that is still a run-on sentence. It is relatively easy to correct this mistake; following are several correct ways to state the same idea.

Whereas Ockeghem usually wrote..., Josquin composed lines that have...
Ockeghem usually wrote...; Josquin, however, composed lines that have...
Ockeghem usually wrote...no clear phrase structure. Josquin, on the other hand, composed lines that have...

Note that is is always possible to break a run-on sentence into two sentences. If you want to keep the two clauses in one sentence, you have two choices. You can either form a compound sentence by keeping the two main clauses and separating them with either a conjunction or a semicolon, or form a complex sentence by turning one into a subordinate clause and keeping the other as the main clause. In a complex sentence, a comma is sufficient punctuation between the two clauses.

Singular Subject, Singular Verb; Plural Subject, Plural Verb

One of the fundamental rules in most languages is that the subject and the verb must agree in number. Students break this basic rule with surprising frequency, usually in long and unwieldy constructions that blur the identity of the real subject. Consider the following sentence.

No innovative composer, not even the twentieth-century composers usually classified as members of the avant-garde, such as Cage, Stockhausen, and Wuorinen, have ever totally abandoned their musical roots.

What happens here is that the singular subject ("No composer") gets buried under the subsequent verbiage, with its plural nouns and the series of names, so that the writer is thinking in the plural by the time he or she gets to the verb. If one corrects the sentence, changing to a singular verb (*"has* ever totally abandoned his musical roots"), the sentence is correct but sounds awkward and ungainly. In such a situation, cross out the whole thing and start again, first forming a clearer idea of exactly what you want to say.

Proper Cases of Pronouns

There is a tendency among some student writers to choose forms of pronouns by sound rather than thinking about the grammatical function of the pronoun in the context. This error occurs especially in compound phrases, like the following.

My parents frequently took my brother and I to concerts and plays.

Since *I* is the object of the verb *took,* it should be in the objective case, *me.* People who would never say "took I to concerts" somehow feel that "my brother and I" is always more correct than "my brother and me," whatever case is required by the context. If you have trouble deciding the correct form in sentences like this, review the simple rules about the proper cases of pronouns.

The Dangler

Another common error is the "dangler," or dangling participle, with no appropriate noun nearby for it to modify. Here is an example from the editorial page of a major newspaper.

In 1961, while sitting at my desk in the White House reflecting on the future of the great Republic, a secretary interrupted with a phone call...

As that sentence stands, the *secretary* was sitting at the writer's desk and reflecting when she interrupted him. *Sitting* and *reflecting* are participles, which function as both verbs and adjectives. When a participle begins a phrase or a sentence, it must modify the subject of the main clause. At best, danglers make a sentence meaningless; at worst, as in this example, they can create a comical effect. A dangling participle need not appear at the beginning of a sentence; here is a reverse dangler, with the participle at the end, from a student's concert report.

The "Stabat Mater" seems to be a very popular text for composers, having heard Pergolesi's setting just last month in a Philharmonic concert.

Obviously, the student meant that *she* had heard Pergolesi's setting performed just last month, but as the sentence stands, "having heard" refers to the subject of the sentence, "Stabat Mater."

In papers about music, one frequently sees sentences like the following.

Turning to the second movement, a serene introduction leads to the main body.

As it stands, this sentence means that the introduction is turning to the second movement. Correct ways to state this idea include:

Turning to the second movement, we find . . .
or: In the second movement, a serene introduction . . .

Like run-ons and sentence fragments, danglers result from sloppy thinking, flagging concentration, or some combination of the two.

Mixed Metaphors

Metaphors, comparisons expressed without the word *like* or *as*, can add color and elegance to one's writing. Unfortunately, metaphors are not always easy to control or to sustain for any length of time. One problem that can arise when the writer reaches for colorful comparisons is the *mixed metaphor*, in which several clashing figures of speech are used too close to one another, creating a confused or comical picture in the reader's mind. A journalist, writing about an election campaign, created this interesting mixed metaphor:

It was the sort of last-minute red herring on which an entire election can hinge.

That is a mind-boggling picture—an election hinging on a herring. The writer obviously did not consider the literal meaning of the words he used. In the editorial cited in the discussion of danglers, there was also a wonderful mixed metaphor.

It was my introduction to the world of influence-peddling and corruption that in recent years has grown from a minor if ineradicable stain on political integrity to a mammoth toxic miasma that is polluting the most basic principles of democratic government.

We know what the writer wants to say, and we sense his outrage, but can the reader actually picture a small "stain" growing into a "mammoth toxic miasma"?

One last example illustrates how these strange constructions happen. An attorney, assuring the press that the government had no case against his client, proclaimed, "The whole house of cards is built on sand." Each metaphor makes sense individually; a house of cards and a house built on sand are traditional symbols of instability. The alert reader, however, is thrown off by the startling combination of pictures.

When you venture into metaphor, be sure that the comparison you choose is helpful rather than distracting, stay with a single comparison, be sure that it does not get out of control, and abandon the comparison the instant it no longer serves your purpose.

The Split Infinitive

An old grammatical rule forbids the splitting of an infinitive, as in the following sentence.

His goal in the symphonic poems was to as vividly as possible describe the main ideas or feelings depicted in the story.

The rule states that the infinitive, *to describe*, should not be interrupted by another word or phrase. The correct way to write that sentence is "His goal in the symphonic poems was to describe as vividly as possible..." *or:* "as vividly as possible to describe...."

Some recent books on writing style allow a split infinitive if only one word intervenes between the two halves of the infinitive or if it seems the most graceful way to convey your thought. In formal papers, it is best to keep infinitives together.

SPELLING

English, as we pointed out previously, is a wondrous language, unusually rich in vocabulary and synonyms, but it does have the disadvantage of illogical and inconsistent spelling. When you are writing or editing, have a good dictionary close at hand; one reliable dictionary is the Collegiate Edition of Webster's Third. Look up every spelling about which you have any doubt. There is no way to avoid using a dictionary. Some correctly spelled words always look wrong; if you stare long enough at even the simplest words, they begin to look strange.

One class of words that are frequently misspelled are adjectives or nouns derived from Latin participles. In American English, the final vowels in words like *predominant* and *occurrence* are all pronounced as *schwas* (an "uh" sound). Therefore one cannot spell these words phonetically. Since the choice of vowel depends on the conjugation of the Latin root, the only way to be sure of the spelling, short of learning Latin, is to look it up.

There is no magical path to correct spelling. First, one must take spelling seriously and accept the fact that English spelling is difficult, illogical, and inconsistent. Second, one must buy a good dictionary and use it constantly when writing or editing. Recent editions of standard dictionaries have become more permissive and often list two spellings for the same word. In formal papers, always use the first or preferred spelling.

Possessives

The rule for forming possessives is: Add an apostrophe and an *s* to form the possessive of a singular noun, and an apostrophe to form the possessive of plural nouns, except for plurals that end in letters other than *s*, like *women* and *children*. Current practice in the formation of possessives has changed in one detail. According to the *Chicago Manual of Style* (6.12–23), one should add an apostrophe and an *s* to proper nouns that end in *s* or another sibilant, except for *Jesus*, *Moses*, and multisyllable Greek names ending in *-es*, like *Demosthenes* and *Sophocles*. Thus, in current practice, the following possessives are correct.

Dickens's	Berlioz's
Marx's	Ives's
Burns's	Albeniz's

These possessives, while correct, seem awkward; one can avoid the problem by rewriting the phrase.

the symphonies of Ives (*rather than* Ives's symphonies)
the influence of Berlioz on later program music (*rather than* Berlioz's influence on later program music)

Plurals of Latin and Greek Words

Some students find it difficult to remember the singular and plural forms of borrowed Greek and Latin words. The society at large has the same trouble. Writers forget, for instance, that *data* and *media* are plural, not singular. Thus, one sees sentences like "The media has blown this problem all out of proportion." In order to use these troublesome words correctly, one must either memorize the correct form or consult a trustworthy dictionary and use the preferred form listed first. Following is a list of frequently misused borrowed Greek and Latin words, with their correct singular and plural forms.

SINGULAR	PLURAL
addendum	addenda
alumnus (masculine)	alumni (masculine, or mixed genders)
alumna (feminine)	alumnae (feminine)
crisis	crises
criterion	criteria
curriculum	curricula
datum	data
erratum	errata
medium	media
phenomenon	phenomena
thesis	theses

Foreign Words

Related to the issue of spelling is the question of correct treatment of foreign words. As a general rule, all foreign words are underlined in typescript and set in italics in print. When foreign words are proper nouns or appear within quotation marks, as in a title, then they are *not* underlined, since the quotation marks already set them off from the text.

If you use a dot-matrix printer that can switch easily to an italic typestyle, you may still choose to follow the rules for typing and underline foreign words. The italic type on some printers is too close to the standard type or too distracting to be effective.

Foreign words and names must be copied exactly, with all the appropriate accents, umlauts, tildes, and other diacritical marks. To omit any of these marks is to misspell the word or the name. If your typewriter or printer does not have all the special marks that you need for foreign words, you must add them by hand, using a pen with a fine point and black ink.

Unless you have studied the foreign language in question, it is very difficult to remember the exact nature and location of each accent mark, especially when you are dealing with Slavic names, such as Dvořák, or with long foreign titles, like the French title of Debussy's *Prelude to the Afternoon of a Faun.* Therefore one should consult a reliable reference work, such as the

New Grove or the latest edition of the *Baker's Biographical Dictionary,* and carefully follow the exact spellings found in those resources.

Recently, there have been changes in the standard ways of transliterating names from foreign alphabets. There is a new method of transliterating Chinese, so that we now write *Beijing* instead of *Peking.* There have also been changes in the standard way of transliterating Russian names from the Cyrillic alphabet. One now sees spellings such as *Rakhmaninov* and *Chaikovski,* as well as the older, more Germanic spellings. Generally, when a project focuses on one composer or a few works, one quickly becomes accustomed to the correct spellings and accents of names that occur constantly. The writer must rely on standard reference works and then be rigidly consistent in using one standard spelling.

Medieval and Renaissance Names

Some students have great difficulty with the names of medieval and Renaissance personages, referring incorrectly to "da Vinci" or "de Vitry" as if those were last names. One standard way of naming people in those periods was by given name and place of origin, like "Guillaume de Machaut," "Guido of Arezzo," and "Giovanni Pierluigi da Palestrina." Sometimes people were known by their given name and an *epithet,* or description of something characteristic of them, like "William the Conqueror," "Prince Henry the Navigator," "Richard the Lion-hearted," and "Charles the Bald." Compounding the confusion, medieval and Renaissance names are frequently translated into different languages, so that one can find many different versions of the same name. Petrus de Cruce is sometimes referred to as "Pierre de la Croix," and the Italian Trecento theorist is referred to either by "Marchettus Padovensis," the Latin form of his name, or by "Marchetto da Padua," the Italian version.

Unfortunately, we have not been consistent in referring to these people, so that we commonly speak of "Machaut" as if that were the composer's last name rather than the name of the town in which he was born. In library card catalogs, Machaut is alphabetized correctly under *G* for "Guillaume," whereas Palestrina is found incorrectly under *P.* The only reason that we have been able to use "Machaut" and "Palestrina" as if they were names of specific people is that no one else of any importance ever came from those small towns. We certainly could not use the same system for other places, and write "Aquitaine" for "Eleanor of Aquitaine" (or William of Aquitaine), or use "Paris," "Rome," "Florence," or "London" as the names of specific persons.

When you are working on a project that involves names like these, consult a reliable reference work and be consistent in using the ways of referring to people that you find there.

SOME FREQUENTLY MISUSED WORDS

This section singles out for discussion a few words that are frequently misused in student papers.

Its and It's

It should not be difficult to distinguish the possessive adjective *its* from the contraction *it's*. *Its*, without the apostrophe, is the correct form when the writer means the possessive *of it*, in a sentence like the following.

The contrabassoon is the lowest instrument of the orchestra; its range extends down to the second B-flat below the bass clef.

It's, with an apostrophe, is a contraction of *it is*. *It's* is seldom appropriate in a formal paper, since all contractions are out of place in formal writing. The common error is to write *it's*, with the apostrophe, in situations similar to the sentence above, when *its* is correct.

Whose and Who's

Similar confusion exists between *whose*, the possessive form of the relative pronoun *who*, and *who's*, a contraction of *who is*. The common mistake, as in the case of *its* and *it's*, is to write the contraction instead of the possessive in sentences like the following.

The composer whose works found the widest acceptance . . .

Awareness that contractions are generally out of place in a formal paper will help you to avoid these two errors.

Principal and Principle

There are many pairs of words in English that are easy to confuse. Distinguishing *principal* from *principle* seems to be difficult for many students. *Principal* is generally an adjective meaning "main" or "most important," although it also can be used as a noun meaning "the head of a school" or "an amount of money." *Principle* is a noun meaning "a fundamental law or doctrine." The following sentences illustrate correct use of these similar words.

The principal composer of the late baroque period . . .
She was hired as the principal horn of the Philharmonic.
The new principal of the high school has greatly improved the music program.

A good essay must be based on the principles of unity and coherence.
He is a man of principle.

Only

Only must be placed in a sentence carefully, as close as possible to the word or the idea that it modifies. Study the following sentences; changing the location of *only* changes the meaning completely.

Only I saw her yesterday. (No one else did.)
I only saw her yesterday. (I didn't speak to her or have any other kind of contact with her.)
I saw only her yesterday. (I didn't see anyone else.)
I saw her only yesterday. (I saw her that recently.)

The common error in the use of *only* is to place it too early in the sentence, usually before the verb, when it belongs with a later word or phrase. "I only have eyes for you," the refrain of an old popular song, illustrates this error; the sentence should read, "I have eyes only for you." Consider the following sentences.

Wrong: He only achieved success as a performer late in his life.
Right: He achieved success as a performer only late in his life.

However, Yet, Still, and so on

Since *however* and similar words are adverbs, not conjunctions, they cannot be used with a comma to separate independent clauses. The following sentence is a run-on sentence and must be rewritten.

Haydn worked for the same aristocratic family for most of his life, however Mozart never found a satisfactory patronage situation.

There are several ways to rewrite that sentence so that it is grammatically correct. If one wants to keep the word *however*, it is necessary to put a semicolon between the two clauses or write them as two sentences. Note also that *however* seems more graceful when it is placed in some position other than the opening of the second sentence. Among the correct ways to state these ideas are the following.

Haydn worked for the same aristocratic family for most of his life. Mozart, however, never found a satisfactory patronage position.
Whereas Haydn worked for the same aristocratic family for most of his life, Mozart never found . . .

There are many other ways to write these sentences so that the contrast between the careers of the two composers is made clear. The one thing to avoid is the use of *however* as a conjunction, a role it cannot play.

Relative Pronouns

Students often mix up the relative pronouns *who, which,* and *that.* Each has its distinctive function.

Who is the correct relative pronoun when the antecedent is a person. There are three forms of this relative pronoun: *Who* is the nominative case, *whose* is possessive, and *whom* is objective. The various forms are used correctly in the following sentences.

Ockeghem, who taught many of the younger composers of his time...
The patron in whose service he worked...
The master whom he chose to imitate...

A common error is to use *who* incorrectly as the object of a preposition.

Wrong: The person who he relied on...
Right: The person on whom he relied...

Which and *that* refer to things and sometimes to groups of people when they are considered a collective unit. *Which* is used in nonrestrictive clauses— that is, in clauses that add information about the antecedent rather than specifying it. *That* is used in restrictive clauses, which specify a general subject. Therefore, *that* is usually correct in adjective clauses without commas, and *which* is correct in clauses with commas. The distinction between restrictive and nonrestrictive clauses will come up again in the discussion of commas in the section on punctuation. The following sentences are correct.

Otello, which was one of Verdi's last operas,...
The opera that made Verdi a success was...

If the correct use of relative pronouns in a particular sentence causes problems for you, either consult a reliable writing guide or rewrite the sentence in a simpler form.

Due to and *Because of*

Student writers often confuse *due to* and *because of. Due* is an adjective; therefore, *due to* can be correctly used only after some form of the verb *to be,* as a predicate adjective. *Due to* is never correct at the beginning of a sentence.

Wrong: Due to the troubled political climate in Italy, Verdi constantly had trouble with the Austrian censors.
Right: Because of the troubled political climate in Italy, Verdi constantly had trouble with the Austrian censors.
Right: Verdi's constant trouble with the Austrian censors was due to the troubled political climate in Italy.

The discussion of misused words could go on for several more chapters; we have discussed only a few common errors. Consult one of the style guides for further details.

PUNCTUATION

Correct punctuation is another troublesome area for many student writers. Consult Chapter 5 of the *Chicago Manual of Style* or Part VI of the Simon & Schuster *Handbook* for authoritative discussions of the proper use of punctuation. Here we will mention a few situations that seem to cause problems for students.

The Period

The period is used after every complete sentence. It is also used after abbreviations, like *m.* for "measure," *mm.* for "measures," and *ms.* for "manuscript." All footnotes end with a period. In bibliography entries, a period appears between the author's name and the title, between the title and the publication information, and at the end of the entry. See Chapter 6 for discussion of the proper format for footnotes and bibliographies.

In a typed paper, it is accepted practice to put a space after every period, particularly after periods that follow abbreviations. Thus "m.5" is incorrect, since there is no space following the period; it should be typed as "m. 5."

Note: Many of us were trained to double-space after a period or any other punctuation mark at the end of a sentence. That practice seems to be falling into disuse. The rule appears in Troyka's handbook (Appendix B, Section 1, p. 675) and in many of the older guides, such as Campbell and Irvine, which follow the practice of double-spacing between sentences both in the text and in their illustrations of correct writing. The rule, however, does not appear anywhere in the *Chicago Manual*, as far as I can tell. Word processing may have changed that rule; this practice could cause problems when the writer uses a computer. As always, check with your instructor to see which practice you should follow, or, if free to make your own choice, follow the *Chicago Manual of Style*.

The Comma

Many student writers seem mystified by the comma and its proper use. Some situations seem particularly troublesome.

Series   In a series containing more than two items, commas should separate each item, including the last one.

> The leading composers of the Mannheim school were Johann Stamitz, Ignaz Holzbauer, Christian Cannabich, and Carl Stamitz.

Some style guides now allow the omission of the last comma, before *and,* provided that it is not necessary for clarity. The *Chicago Manual of Style* (5.50) recommends that the writer always include that final comma. If one chooses to omit it, there is always the danger that the last two items will be read as a two-part single item, like Gilbert and Sullivan or Rodgers and Hammerstein. It seems easier to include the last comma as a matter of course than to decide in each case if it is necessary.

Appositives   If a phrase simply tells us something more about a noun, it should be set off by commas.

> Monteverdi's *Orfeo,* an opera in the Florentine style, was first performed in 1607 at the Gonzaga court in Mantua.

If an appositive phrase is restrictive—that is, if it specifies a general noun—then commas are not used.

> Verdi's opera *La Traviata* is based on a novel by Dumas.

If commas were used to set off the title in the preceding sentence, the sentence would imply that *La Traviata* was the only opera Verdi composed.

Restrictive and nonrestrictive clauses   Commas are used to set off nonrestrictive clauses, just as they are used to set off nonrestrictive appositives; commas are not used to set off restrictive clauses.

> The composers who fled from Nazi Germany in the thirties . . .
> Arnold Schoenberg, who fled from Nazi Germany in the thirties, . . .

In the first case, the relative clause is restrictive, making the general noun *composers* more specific; therefore, commas are not used. In the second sentence, the relative clause is nonrestrictive; it adds information rather than making a general subject more specific. Therefore, commas must be used.

Compound and complex sentences A comma is used between the clauses of a compound sentence, provided that they are joined by a conjunction. If the clauses are short and there is no possibility of confusion, the comma may be omitted.

Berg used the twelve-tone system freely to create a style we usually describe as expressionist, but Webern extended the twelve-tone idea into new areas.

A comma is used between the clauses of complex sentences.

Although much of the music of the postwar period can be traced to the influence of Webern, the neoromanticism of recent years can be interpreted as a return to the freer and more expressive style of Berg.

Introductory phrases A comma is generally used after all introductory phrases.

Judging from the correspondence, we can conclude that Brahms was very worried about the first performance of his First Symphony.

If the introductory phrase is short and there is no possibility of misinterpretation, the comma may be omitted.

In 1723 Bach accepted the post of Cantor at the Thomaskirche in Leipzig.

If there is any possibility of confusion or what the *Chicago Manual* calls mistaken junction, the comma should be included to ensure clarity.

Confusing: Soon after the concert was interrupted by loud catcalls and angry denunciations.
Clear: Soon after, the concert was interrupted by loud catcalls and angry denunciations.

Without the comma, "after the concert" can be read as a prepositional phrase, confusing the reader.

The Semicolon

The semicolon marks a more important break in the flow of a sentence than breaks marked by a comma. In particular, the semicolon is used to separate the two parts of a compound sentence when they are not connected by a conjunction.

Stravinsky performed as a pianist and conductor all his life; Schoenberg was a university teacher.

Note that words like *however, thus, yet,* and *hence* are not conjunctions, but adverbs; therefore, a semicolon is necessary between the clauses of a compound sentence when one of these words appears in the second clause.

Stravinsky performed as a pianist and conductor all his life; Schoenberg, however, was a university professor.

When items in a series are long and complex or contain internal commas, semicolons are used to separate the items.

Among Verdi's most popular works are *Rigoletto,* produced in Venice in 1851; *La Traviata,* produced in Venice in 1853; and *Aïda,* produced in Cairo in 1871.

The Colon

The colon is used to mark a greater break in the flow of a sentence than breaks marked by the semicolon. In expository prose, the colon has two main uses. The first is to introduce a formal statement or quotation.

The rule may be stated thus: Material that appears in the dominant or in another related key in the exposition...
He answered as follows: No prince may force me to compose at his whim.

The colon is also used to introduce lists.

Rosen's book deals with the composers whom he views as the chief exponents of the Classical style: Haydn, Mozart, and Beethoven.

Quotations Marks

In Chapter 6 we discussed the proper format for brief and long quotations and the conventions one should follow when citing the words of someone else. You may want to review that section. Here we need to add a few rules about quotation marks in combination with other kinds of punctuation. Note that American practice diverges from British practice in this matter; we will explain American practice.

1. Periods and commas required by the context of the sentence are placed *inside* the quotation marks, whether or not the period or the comma is part of the quoted material. Logical or not, the following sentences are correctly punctuated.

At the conclusion of "Sempre libera," we know much more about Violetta's character and her ambivalence about love.
A striking example of Ives's technique of quotation is "Decoration Day."

2. Semicolons, colons, question marks, and exclamation points required by the context of the sentence are placed *outside* quotation marks. Thus:

A good example of his collage technique is "Decoration Day"; a clear example of his impressionist style is "The Housatonic at Stockbridge."

The Hyphen

The hyphens is used to divide the first part of a word at the end of a line from the second part at the beginning of the next line. Students frequently err in the way they divide words. Short or one-syllable words may not be divided; longer words may be divided, provided that you follow the rules for dividing words correctly. Consult a dictionary to check the proper division of words, or simply start the word on the next line.

Hyphens are also used in constructions like *two-voice, one-syllable, fast-moving,* and *long-neglected.* Accepted practice is not consistent in the use or omission of hyphens in these constructions; one must consult a dictionary to be certain.

The so-called suspended hyphen in compound constructions can be confusing and should be used with great care. It is correct to write "in three- and four-voice polyphony," meaning "in three-voice and four-voice polyphony," but be careful that your meaning is clear.

The Dash

Dashes can be used in expository prose to interrupt a sentence's structure to add information, such as a definition, an explanation, or a reaction or comment. Although this construction should be used with restraint, it can be effective.

The composers of the late madrigal—Marenzio, Monteverdi, and Gesualdo—based their musical style on rhetorical effects.

Note that there are several other ways to convey that idea without using the dashes. Note also that in typing, a dash is *two hyphens,* with no space before or after. Do not use a single hyphen or the underline character in place of a two-hyphen dash.

Parentheses

Parentheses are used to enclose additional information that breaks up the flow of the sentence. The common error regarding parentheses is to overuse them. If the material is important, include it somehow in the text without parentheses. If it is not important, leave it out, or put it in a footnote. Constant use of parentheses means that the writer has not thought out clearly what he or she wants to say and uses the parentheses to include last-minute additions.

There are many other rules about punctuation. There is no need to discuss exclamation points here, since they are of little use in expository prose. Experience with student papers shows that the most critical need is for students to learn the correct use of the comma, rather than following the random and guesswork systems they seem to use now. For further details of correct punctuation, consult Chapter 5 of the *Chicago Manual of Style* or Part VI of the *Simon & Schuster Handbook for Writers*.

SPECIAL PROBLEMS INVOLVED IN WRITING ABOUT MUSIC

Writing about music involves a special set of technical problems, which confuse some students. We will discuss a few of the common ones.

Historical and Stylistic Terms

There are two main ways to deal with the standard names for historical periods. One uses uppercase letters for the terms when they mean a definite historical period, and lowercase letters when they are used in a more general sense.

the Middle Ages
the Renaissance
the Baroque Era, *but* baroque decoration
the Classical symphony, *but* classical music (as opposed to popular music)
Romantic music, *but* a romantic view of nature
the Twentieth Century

The *Chicago Manual of Style* (7.61) recommends uppercase letters only for the Middle Ages, the Renaissance, and similar specific periods, like the Age of Reason or the Enlightenment; all other such designations are not capitalized. Thus, baroque, classic or classical, romantic, neoclassic or neo-classicism, impressionism, and similar terms are now lowercase unless they are proper nouns, like "Victorian." This second style is followed in this book, and I recommend that student writers follow this practice, unless their instructors specify otherwise.

Titles of Works

Naming musical works correctly is not always easy. Often the writer must consult reliable reference works to find the correct title for a work. Here are some general principles.

Quotation marks or italics? In general, titles of individual selections within larger works are put in quotation marks; titles of larger works are set in italics—underlined in typescript.

"Come scoglio" from *Così fan tutte*
"Decoration Day" from the *Holidays Symphony*
"Um Mitternacht" from the *Mörike Lieder*
"I Know that my Redeemer Liveth" from *Messiah*

Note that this rule supersedes the general rule about italicizing (underlining) all foreign words. Generally, foreign words inside quotation marks are not underlined.

Generic titles Generic titles are capitalized when they name specific works and are left in lowercase when the terms are used in their generic sense.

Haydn's Symphony No. 104 ("London")
The symphonies of Haydn

Translating foreign titles If a work that you refer to frequently has both a foreign title and a commonly used English title, it is permissible to use the translated title after the first reference. If there is only a single reference to a work, use the foreign title.

Die Walküre (rather than *The Valkyries*)
Le Sacre du printemps (rather than *The Rite of Spring*)
Also sprach Zarathustra (rather than *Thus Spake Zarathustra*)

The correct order of complex titles We discussed proper ways to cite titles of works in Chapter 6. The correct order of elements in a title can be confusing, particularly in the case of generic titles that also include keys, opus numbers, catalog numbers, and subtitles. The only sure way to deal with this question is to consult reliable reference works and consistently follow the order and punctuation given there. The main goals are always clarity and consistency.

Naming Notes and Keys

There are many ways to refer to specific notes and keys in a paper about music; some are clearer than others. Notes should be listed in capital letters and underlined when there is any danger of their being mistaken for words of text. When referring to keys in papers, students sometimes use the conventional system for graphic analyses, in which capital *E* stands for "E major" and lowercase *e* stands for "E minor." In a paper, that system can be confusing for the reader. It is better to write "E major" and "E minor," always using the uppercase letter and writing out the mode. Write "E-flat," with the hyphen and with *flat* spelled out, rather than "E♭" or "F♯", which can be confusing to the eye. When keys are specified in titles, *major* and *minor* should be capitalized: "Piano Concerto in F Minor."

Foreign Words

Underlining   As a rule, foreign words should be underlined in a typed paper. The problem with musical terms is that some foreign words have ceased to be foreign. By now, words like *sonata, concerto,* and *ostinato,* originally Italian words, have become standard English words and need not be treated as foreign terms. On the other hand, some compounds of those terms, like *sonata da chiesa* and *concerto grosso,* are still treated as foreign terms and thus should be underlined. If you do not know if a term is regarded as standard English, consult a reliable reference work and see how that work treats the term. If the word appears in a standard English dictionary, it can be treated as an English word.

Some terms have not only been adopted into standard English, but have also been shortened in the process. *Violoncello,* for instance, originally an Italian word, has become an English word, usually shortened to *cello.* I see no reason to insist on the longer form; both *violoncello* and *'cello,* with the apostrophe indicating that the word used to be longer, now seem affected. If you use the long form, be sure to spell it correctly; *violincello* is wrong. Consistency is the main requirement, in the question of technical terms as in so many other cases.

Plural forms of foreign words   The correct plural forms of foreign words can be difficult. If the word is regarded as a foreign term, then its plural ought to be formed by following the rules of the foreign language.

SINGULAR	PLURAL
Lied	*Lieder*
primo uomo	*primi uomi*
prima donna	*prime donne*

comprimario	*comprimarii*
tromba	*trombe*
corno da caccia	*corni da caccia*
sinfonia	*sinfonie*

Sometimes a generic musical term has become standard English, while a particular specific form of the term is still regarded as a foreign term. In those cases, the plurals of the generic terms should follow English rules, while the plural forms of the foreign terms should follow the rules of the foreign language. Thus:

sonatas	but *sonate da chiesa, sonate da camera*
concertos	but *concerti grossi*
violas	but *viole da gamba*
violins	but *violini piccoli*

It may seem pedantic to insist on these foreign plural forms, but there is no sensible alternative. If you decide that *concerto grosso* has become an English term, how would you form the plural? Concertos grosso? Concerto grossos? There are other plurals, like *oboes d'amore*, that may look strange on the page. If you are not comfortable writing these plural forms, there are two courses of action open to you. First, you can consult a musical dictionary or another reference work in order to find the correct plural form. Second, you can rewrite the sentence so that you do not need to use the plural form.

Sonate da chiesa differ from *sonate da camera* in several respects.

This sentence can easily be rewritten as follows:

A *sonata da chiesa* typically differs from a *sonata da camera* in several respects.

Technical Terms

Imprecise use of technical terms is a common source of errors in student papers. There are two common ways in which technical terms are misused. The first is to confuse similar terms. For example, there are several related terms that one can use to describe a polyphonic texture that is imitative. *Imitation, canon, fugato,* and *fugue* all describe types of imitative technique, but each means something different. The second error, especially in discussions of early music, is to apply terms applicable to one style of music to a style that is substantially different. Like any technical field, analysis has its specialized vocabulary, essential for discussing musical analysis, and these technical terms must be used precisely and carefully. To avoid confusion, remember that if you are using a particular word as a technical musical term, you should not use it in its more general English sense.

Describing Musical Events

We pointed out earlier that it is not easy to describe musical events. Finding a clear way of expressing what occurs in a musical work is sometimes a difficult challenge. Three particular questions deserve discussion.

Subjects and verbs   One area to consider carefully is how to describe what happens in a musical work. If you want to describe a striking cadenza in a violin concerto, for example, there are several ways of stating your idea. Consider the following sentences.

> The solo violin embarks on a brilliant exploration of motives taken from the first theme.
>
> The composer turns the soloist loose in a brilliant cadenza based on motives taken from the first theme.
>
> Motives taken from the first theme are woven into a brilliant cadenza.

None of these descriptions is completely satisfactory. The first seems to ascribe the cadenza to the instrument rather than to the composer or the soloist; the second seems to overpersonalize the interaction between composer and interpreter; the third falls into the stale passive voice. Perhaps the following versions are more suitable.

> A brilliant cadenza for the soloist continues to explore motives taken from the first theme.
>
> The soloist then plays a brilliant cadenza based on motives taken from the first theme.

Experiment with several versions of musical description until you find one that avoids the multiple pitfalls of pretentious language, overly personal description, and weak passive voice constructions.

Confusion of tenses   Students often fall into confusion in choosing the proper tense of the verbs they use to describe musical events. In general, the present tense is appropriate when the reader's attention is focused on the music itself. If the emphasis is on the composer's act of creating the music or on the details of a particular performance, the past tense is appropriate. Consider the following sentences.

In the opening chorus of Cantata No. 4, the sopranos sing the chorale melody in long notes, while the other voices sing free counterpoint.

In the opening chorus of Cantata No. 4, Bach assigned the chorale tune to the sopranos and composed free counterpoint for the other voices.

At the end of the coda, the brass section repeats the main theme once more, bringing this long movement to a dramatic conclusion.

In typical Romantic fashion, Liszt chose to restate the main theme once more at the end of the coda, assigning it to the brass section.

One sees statements like "Bach assigns the chorale tune to the sopranos," but that wording is jarring—after all, Bach died a long time ago. Even when describing ongoing or repeated actions that took place in the past, the past tense makes better sense than the present.

Schubert consistently chose the texts for his songs from the works of a few favorite poets.

Bach based many of his cantatas on the chorale tunes that had been traditional in the Lutheran church for two hundred years.

Another error is to use both present and past tense in the same sentence or paragraph. If you start by using the present tense, with the emphasis on what happens in the music rather than on the composer's choices, you should stay with that focus and that tense. Constant vacillation between present and past tense is confusing.

Finding appropriate ways to state qualitative judgments   Another challenge in writing about music, or any art, is finding appropriate ways to state qualitative judgments. It is not enough for the writer to label everything "beautiful." The writer must search through the huge store of synonyms in the English language to find the exact word that says what he or she wants to say. The weakest possible critical term is *interesting;* that is what one mumbles when standing, baffled, in front of the latest avant-garde artwork. On the other hand, words like *stirring, dramatic,* or *chilling,* which may be appropriate to describe late romantic works, might very well be taken as insults by avant-garde composers of the late twentieth century. *Fascinating, challenging, intriguing,* and *complex* may be more appropriate descriptions for some styles of music.

It takes thought and creativity to come up with exactly the right word to describe the aesthetic effect of a particular piece of music. One wants to avoid both extremes—dull words like *interesting,* and affected or pretentious language. Finding the right evaluative word to use in your summary or conclusion may seem to be the most difficult part of writing a paper, but it is worth the struggle to find the one word that will say exactly what you want to say and provide a strong, effective conclusion.

CONCLUSION

This chapter has discussed some writing problems that mar student writing in any field and the special problems of writing about music. The advice is intended to provide practical assistance. If you approach your writing assignments armed with an awareness of common writing errors and ways to avoid them, your task should be easier. You should be able to write and edit your work with a greater sense of security, confident that your papers will have a better chance of being taken seriously as representative of the high quality of your work.

Conclusion

Since the purpose of this book is to provide practical advice about writing in general, and writing about music in particular, the emphasis, particularly in Chapters 3–14, has been on the mechanics and technical details of writing. These details are important; carelessness about these seemingly minor matters can defeat the writer's goal of communicating important ideas to the reader. The unifying theme of this book, running through all the discussions of details, is that effective writing takes time, care, and precision. Every step in the process of writing a paper—research, drafting, editing, and final typing—demands that the writer understand what he or she is doing and expend the necessary time and effort to do things in the proper way. The writer must take sufficient pride in his or her work to care about technical matters like proper format, correct spelling, and careful editing. Students will never succeed in their writing assignments until they develop a competent and professional prose style.

It is time now to step back from the details and return to the larger perspective with which the book began. Effective and careful writing can vastly improve a paper, whereas an incompetent and careless writing style can destroy the effectiveness of a paper.

Important as it is to develop a competent and effective writing style, however, a good writing style is not enough in itself to produce effective prose about music. The ability to write clear, effective prose is only a means of communicating the writer's insight and vision about the art of music. To write well about music the writer needs two different things—vision and insight about music, and the writing skill to communicate that vision clearly and effectively. Unless the writer has the analytical skills to understand a musical work, the aesthetic sensitivity to appreciate its beauty, and the historical insight to understand its significance in the history of music, all the writing skill in the world will not produce prose worth reading. One needs to have both something to say and the skill to say it clearly and forcefully. I have presumed throughout this book that the student writer has something to say; my mission has been to provide practical assistance in the craft of saying it clearly.

I want to close with a plea to all students: Read as many books and articles about music as you can. Read voraciously. After you read the books and articles that you must read in connection with your classes, read everything else you can. Read widely but *critically*, with one eye on the content and one eye on the writing style. When you come across a writer whose style impresses you with its clarity and eloquence, look for other writings by the same author, no matter what the subject, so that you can find out what makes his or her writing style effective. Find models that impress you, and try to isolate exactly what it is about this writer's work that makes it so clear and enjoyable to read. Learn from all your reading, and continue to read with an eye on writing style, looking for ways to improve the clarity and effectiveness of your own writing. Improving your writing is a lifelong task, one that is never finished, but every effort to improve your writing even in a small way will make your writing more effective.

Appendix

Sample Paper

The Appendix contains a paper written by a student. In it you can see how the correct format for footnotes and bibliography works in practice. No paper is perfect; this one needs more footnotes in the section on background. The writer felt that prospective readers would understand that the background information came from standard sources, "common knowledge" among those who work in the classic period. The title page may vary from the format required by your instructor, and the notes are placed at the end of the paper rather than at the bottom of each page. Other than that, however, you can trust the format followed here.

This paper is a solid piece of work. The writer fills in the necessary information about background, the definition of the genre in question, and the circumstances that led to this composition. More important, she discusses the music in a way that helps the reader understand and appreciate this particular work.

HAYDN'S SYMPHONIE CONCERTANTE IN B-FLAT:

BACKGROUND AND ANALYSIS

Silvia Herzog

MuHL 576

Summer, 1986

Were it not for the contributions of Haydn and Mozart, the revered masters of the Classical era, the genre of the symphonie concertante might have been forgotten along with the genre's most prolific composer, Giovanni Giuseppe Cambini. There are, however, two examples by Mozart, one of which survives only in a manuscript of dubious authenticity, and one by Haydn. These three works invite further examination of the symphonie concertante as one of the staple genres of the Classical repertoire. Furthermore, the example by Haydn provides insight into the events surrounding his first visit to London, where the symphonie concertante was very much in fashion.

The symphonie concertante is one of a number of Classical genres that are difficult to define precisely. Like "divertimento," the term "symphonie concertante" seems to be a graceful and easily defined term. Attempts to provide precise descriptions of the genre, however, such as Barry Brook's discussion,[1] necessitate the listing of more exceptions than common elements.

The genres that the symphonie concertante is said to resemble most closely include the symphony, the concerto grosso, the Classical concerto, and the divertimento. While it may draw elements from each of these forms, the symphonie concertante is unique. The only valid generalization one can make is that it is a multi-movement form for two or more solo instruments and orchestra.

Many other terms are applied to works in essentially the same form: concertino, concertone, duet concertino, duetto concerto, fantasie concertante, divertimento concertante, concerto concertante, concertierende Sinfonien für verschiedene Instrumente, Gruppen-Konzert, and Konzert-Sinfonie. Haydn entitled his London work Concertante.

The symphonie concertante was a familiar genre in concert programs at this time in both Mannheim and London. It had first emerged as a specific genre, clearly separated from both the symphony and the concerto, in Paris in the 1770's, as a result of the popularity of the form at the Concerts spirituels. We know of at least 130 French composers of symphonies concertantes; the composers of this genre from Mannheim and London wrote these pieces for the Paris concert series.

Among the important French composers of symphonies concertantes are Breval, Devienne, Gossec, Saint-Georges, and Chretien. The prolific Italian Cambini, who wrote eighty symphonies concertantes, and the Austrian Pleyel can be grouped with the French composers, since they lived and worked in Paris. Mannheimers who contributed to the genre include Cannabich, Holzbauer, Danzi, and Stamitz, who wrote thirty symphonies concertantes. In London, the prominent composers

were J.C. Bach and Carl Abel, whose works were performed at
both the Bach-Abel Concerts and the Concerts spirituels.[3]

The symphony and the concerto are the main sources from
which the style of the symphonie concertante was derived.
Another important influence, Italian operatic aria and
recitative, is sometimes mentioned in passing, but was clearly
an important influence on many of the works of Cambini,
Stamitz, Pleyel, and Abel. In Haydn's one symphonie
concertante, as we shall see, Italian opera seems to be at
least as important an influence as the symphony and the
concerto.

Haydn's turning to this genre was not a logical result of
his continued stylistic growth. In fact, the form is an
anomaly in the context of his works of this period. He
composed his symphonie concertante in 1792, at the same time
as the symphonies written for the Salomon Concerts in London.
Since the symphonie concertante is so different from these
other works, one wonders why he tried his hand at this genre.

The first clearly documented attempt to persuade Haydn to
visit London was made by Willoughby Bertie, Fourth Earl of
Abington, in 1782. It is possible that, even earlier, Johann
Christian Bach and Carl Abel may have invited Haydn to London;
he declined the invitation, and sent along a version of
Symphony No. 53 with a newly composed final movement to be
performed in their concert series. Other invitations were
issued by Wilhelm Cramer in 1785, the impresario Gallini in

1786, Mr. Hammersley in 1787, Gaetano Bartolozzi in 1787, and
the publisher John Bland in 1789. They all failed. Finally,
Johann Peter Salomon succeeded in bringing "the Shakespeare of
Music" to Great Britain, "the country for which his music
seems to be made."[4] Salomon had severed his relationship with
the popular Professional Concerts and established his own
concert series.

Other factors besides the influence of Salomon affected
Haydn's decision to visit London. His patron Prince Nicholas
died in 1790. After the death of Nicholas, Haydn no longer
felt obliged by loyalty to stay at Esterhaza, where he had
already been tied down too long.

On December 15, 1790, less than three months after the
death of Nicholas, Haydn journeyed to London with Salomon.[5]
This was the first trip abroad for a man who had spent all his
life within the boundaries of German-speaking principalities.

For a man of fifty-eight, Haydn adapted easily to the
inconveniences of travel and a foreign language, and he soon
was involved in the busy musical life of London. There were
five different subscription series of orchestral concerts
taking place simultaneously. The halls were filled to capacity
with enthusiastic patrons who knew about Haydn and were
anxious to attend performances of his music. For the first
time in his career, Haydn felt truly valued and understood.

Haydn's popularity and his association with Salomon
fueled the fires of rivalry between the Salomon Concerts and

the Professional Concerts run by the violinist Wilhelm Cramer.
After a number of successful concerts in Salomon's series,
members of the Professional Concerts tried to attract Haydn to
their series with the promise of more money. When he refused,
they circulated scurrilous rumors about him; they claimed that
he was too old to have any creative genius left. They also
threatened to outdo the Salomon Concerts by engaging for their
series Haydn's pupil Ignaz Pleyel.

Haydn was hurt by these tactics, but, when Pleyel arrived
and acted with the humility appropriate to a student dealing
with his revered master, Haydn accepted his presence
graciously, and the two composers were seen together regularly
at dinners and concerts.

On February 27, 1791, the Professional Concerts presented
a program featuring Pleyel's Sinfonie Concertante in F Major,
Op. 65.[6] Haydn attended the performance with Pleyel, and it is
conceivable that Haydn decided to write his own symphonie
concertante on that evening. The performance of Haydn's
symphonie concertante took place at the competing Salomon
concerts on March 9, 1791, only ten days after he heard
Pleyel's work.[7] The autograph demonstrates that the work was
composed in considerable haste. Further evidence in support of
the theory that Haydn composed his work in response to
Pleyel's can be found in a letter to Maria Anna von Genzinger,
in which the composer complains of the pressure to produce new
works in response to Pleyel's new works.

> There isn't a day, not a single day, in which I am free
> from work, and I shall thank the dear Lord when I can
> leave London--the sooner the better. My labours have been
> augmented by the arrival of my pupil Pleyel, whom the
> Professional Concerts have brought here. He arrived here
> with a lot of new compositions, but they had been
> composed long ago; he therefore promised to present a new
> work every evening. As soon as I saw this, I realized at
> once that a lot of people were dead set against me, and
> so I announced publicly that I would likewise produce
> twelve different new pieces. In order to keep my word,
> and to support poor Salomon, I must be the victim and
> work the whole time. But I really do feel it. My eyes
> suffer the most, and I have many sleepless nights, though
> with God's help I shall overcome it all.8

That Haydn, under such pressure, should choose to write a
symphonie concertante can only be the result of the Pleyel
work. Haydn had never written a piece such as this, and even
the concerto, a close kin to the symphonie concertante, held
little appeal for him. His symphonies, however, provide
evidence for his ability to write in the soloistic way
necessary for this new genre.

It is quite likely that Haydn had never heard the term
"symphonie concertante" when in 1761 he anticipated its
essence in his triptych Le matin, Le midi, and Le soir,
Symphonies No. 6, 7, and 8. These works abound in extended
difficult solo passages that detach themselves from the
orchestral fabric. Le soir is subtitled "à piu stromenti
concertandi,"9 but these are symphonies with solo parts, in
which the relationship of solos to tutti is flexible and
unformalized, unlike that of the true symphonie concertante.

All three works are notable for their many concertante
features; demanding solos are given to flute, bassoon, first

violin, cello, and violone. There are even solos for the principal second violin. In Symphony No. 6, the concertante parts are nominally for violin, cello, and violone, but the bassoon has a part in the Trio of the third movement that is almost as important as that of the bass. In No. 7, there are two flutes that have leading parts after a curious Adagio in recitative style. The first violin, second violin, cello, and violone have solos, and the oboes and bassoon have isolated and demanding episodes. In No. 8, there are copious concertante parts as in No. 7, and the slow movement is nearly a symphonie concertante between two violins, cello, and bassoon.

Symphonies No. 31 and No. 72 show a return to the concertante principles of the early Esterhaza symphonies. In Symphony No. 31 (1765), the concertmaster has a florid solo in the Adagio, and all the other movements have a solo flute. While the concertante parts are predictably shared between various principals by the division into variations in the Finale, it is interesting to note the inclusion of the violone as a soloist once more. This same plan provides the basic arrangement for Symphony No. 72 (1778).

After the experience of composing these soloistic symphonies, and influenced by the example of Pleyel, Haydn proceeded to compose his only symphonie concertante. It is a light-hearted work, somewhat limited in the virtuosity he demands of the solo players, since he frequently uses all the

solo forces simultaneously. Throughout this work, Haydn
reveals his penchant for unconventionality and wit.

The orchestral introduction opens with four similar four-
measure phrases. After arrival at the dominant, the soloists
interrupt at measure 18,[10] introducing a new idea derived from
the first phrase but creating a contrast in mood. The
orchestral introduction continues with another interruption
by the soloists at m. 41. Finally at m. 49, the soloists make
their official entrance. Everything proceeds rather
conventionally until m. 101, where the soloists play an
eleven-measure cadenza passage. An orchestral tutti closes the
exposition on the dominant at m. 126.

The development begins not on the dominant or the
relative minor, but on D-flat; this sudden move to a key area
a third away from the expected one is a device found
frequently in Haydn's piano works as well as in the later
quartets, such as Op. 71 and Op. 73. The development proceeds
upwards first by whole steps, from D-flat in m. 128, through
E-flat minor in m. 134, to F minor in m. 138. Here the
movement proceeds upwards by fifths, with a brief excursion to
the related key of C minor at m. 140, arriving at G minor in
m. 145. Up to this point, the development has utilized
material from the exposition. By the time we arrive at G
minor, a resonable key for developmental activity in a work in
B-flat major, the melodic material is not related at all to the
melodic material of the exposition.

The autograph score contains an additional thirty-six
measures between mm. 158 and 159 of the final version. This
material, which was deleted before the completion of the first
draft, further confirms the key of G minor but continues to
obscure the melodic ideas of the exposition. Instead, we are
left with a tutti at m. 160, which emphasizes the dominant of
G minor, a fermata marking the end of the development, and the
recapitulation at m. 163.

The recapitulation begins with a perfect repetition of
the opening measures. After seventeen measures, the material
is slightly varied, still serving its essential purpose of
emphasizing the tonic. At m. 219, there is a fermata like the
one at m. 101, after which we expect to hear a typical
cadenza. Immediately after the fermata, the soloists enter on
an unexpected D-flat chord, perhaps anticipating the material
later in the piece in the key of D-flat. At m. 219, there is
an unexpected G-flat chord, the surprising chord in an
otherwise harmonically normal cadenza which actually begins at
m. 229.

The bassoon and cello begin immediately with the pastoral
theme of the Andante movement. The unusual feature of
this movement is that the soloists alone carry the weight of
the entire movement. Only once at m. 33 is there a brief
outburst by the orchestra to signal the return of the main
theme, the recapitulation if we view this movement as a
sonatina in structure.

The spritely rondo theme of the third movement, in B-flat, is announced in unison by the entire ensemble. In keeping with his reputation for wit and surprise, Haydn interrupts the rondo theme before it develops into a proper melody with the most curious feature of this entire work, an instrumental recitative for the solo violin. The effect is comical, introducing M. Salomon, the patron of Haydn's visit to London and the violin soloist at these performances, in the unexpected role of an impassioned Italian diva.

[Concertante: Finale] 11

The instrumental recitative in this work does not represent a new device for Haydn. It is a procedure that can be found in Haydn's earliest works for Prince Paul Anton Esterhazy in 1761, the Divertimento à nove stromenti (II: 17) in C for clarinets, horns, and strings, and the Symphony No. 7 ("Le midi"), both of which have elaborate mocking recitatives. In the Divertimento, the recitative appears in the third movement; in the symphony, in the second. There are also examples of this sort in some of the early string quartets,

although, with the exception of Op. 17, No. 5, they are not
clearly marked as recitatives in the score.

The curious thing about the inclusion of this particular
recitative is that, at this point in Haydn's career, he had
already acknowledged that opera was not a form suited to his
talents, and he was in fact weary of the whole idea of opera.

There are no other instances of instrumental recitative
in his later works; one must therefore presume that once again
the influence of Pleyel affected his compositional choices.
Pleyel's own works in this genre abound in operatic passages,
as do the works by his contemporaries from Paris. In those
works, however, it is the aria that is borrowed for the
instrumental writing. Perhaps Haydn's pompous bursts of
recitative were his way of poking fun at Pleyel and the
tradition of the symphonie concertante.

It is plausible to conclude that the historical
importance of this work lies in this odd passage of
recitative, which may have served as the inspiration for the
great double-bass recitative in Beethoven's Ninth Symphony.
Whether or not that possibility is true, the Symphonie
Concertante survives as an example of nostalgic Haydn, relying
on his earlier practices. It also exemplifies all the charm
and wit of his later works, such as the "Oxford" Symphony.

NOTES

1. Barry S. Brook, "Symphonie Concertante," in The New Grove Dictionary of Music and Musicians (London: Macmillan, 1980), Vol. XV, p. 433.

2. Ibid., p. 434.

3. Barry S. Brook, "The Symphonie Concertante: An Interim Report," Musical Quarterly 17 (1961), pp. 506-516.

4. Christopher Roscoe, "Haydn and London in the 1700's," Music and Letters 49 (1968), p. 212.

5. Karl Geiringer, Haydn: A Creative Life in Music (New York: W. W. Norton and Co., 1946; later editions, University of California Press, 1968 and 1982), p. 104.

6. H.C. Robbins Landon, Haydn: Chronicle and Works (Bloomington: University of Indiana Press, 1976), p. 138.

7. Ibid., p. 144.

8. H.C. Robbins Landon, The Collected Correspondence and London Notebooks of Joseph Haydn (London: Barrie and Rockcliff, 1959), p. 132.

9. Anthony van Hoboken, Joseph Haydn: Thematisches-bibliographisches Werkverzeichnis (Mainz: Schott, 1957-1978), Vol. I, p. 48.

10. Measure numbers are from H.C. Robbins Landon, ed., Joseph Haydn: Critical Edition of the Complete Symphonies (Vienna: Universal, 1965), Vol. X, pp. 287-369.

11. Robbins Landon, Chronicles, p. 539.

BIBLIOGRAPHY

Benton, Rita. "Pleyel," in The New Grove Dictionary of Music
and Musicians. London: Macmillan, 1980. Vol. 15,
pp. 264-269.

-------. Thematic Index to the Works of Ignaz Pleyel. New
York: Pendragon Press, 1977.

Brook, Barry S. La Symphonie Française dans la second moitiè
du XVIII siècle. Paris: L'Institut de Musicologie, 1962.

-------. "Symphonie concertante," in The New Grove Dictionary
of Music and Musicians. London: Macmillan, 1980. Vol. 18,
pp. 433-438.

-------. "The Symphonie Concertante: An Interim Report."
Musical Quarterly 47 (1961), pp. 493-516; 48 (1962), p.
148.

-------. "The Symphonie Concertante: Its Musical and
Sociological Bases." International Review of the
Aesthetics and Sociology of Music, 6 (1975), pp. 9-27.

-------. The Symphony, 1720-1840: A Comprehensive Collection
of Full Scores in Sixty Volumes. New York: Garland, 1981.
Series D, Vol. 6.

Geiringer, Karl. Haydn: A Creative Life in Music. New York:
W. W. Norton and Co., 1946; later editions, University of
California Press, 1968 and 1982.

Hoboken, Anthony van. Joseph Haydn: Thematisches-
bibliographisches Werkverzeichnis. Three volumes. Mainz:
Schott, 1957-78.

Hodgson, Antony. The Music of Joseph Haydn: The Symphonies.
London: Tantivy Press, 1976.

Larsen, Jens Peter. The New Grove Haydn. New York: W. W.
Norton and Co., 1982.

-------, Howard Serwer, and James Webster, eds. Haydn Studies:
Proceedings of the International Haydn Conference,
Washington, D.C., 1975.

Robbins Landon, H.C., ed. The Collected Correspondence and
London Notebooks of Joseph Haydn. London: Barrie and
Rockcliff, 1959.

-------, ed. Joseph Haydn: Critical Edition of the Complete Symphonies. Twelve volumes. Vienna: Universal, 1965.

-------. Haydn: Chronicle and Works. Five volumes. Bloomington: Indiana University Press, 1976.

-------. The Symphonies of Joseph Haydn. London: Universal and Rockcliff, 1955.

Roscoe, Christopher. "Haydn and London in the 1700's." Music and Letters 8 (1968), p. 203.

Rosen, Charles. The Classical Style: Haydn, Mozart, Beethoven. New York: W. W. Norton and Co., 1972.

Webster, James. "Towards a History of Viennese Chamber Music in the Early Classical Period." Journal of the American Musicological Society 27 (1974), pp. 212-247.

Wellesz, Egon, and Frederick Sternfeld, eds. The Age of Enlightenment: 1745-1790. New Oxford History of Music, Volume 7. London: Oxford University Press, 1973.

Index